Wayne
KZ6718
Maogoto
author

Technology and the law on the use of force

Technology and the Law on the Use of Force

As governmental and non-governmental operations become progressively supported by vast automated systems and electronic data flows, attacks of government information infrastructure, operations and processes pose a serious threat to economic and military interests. In 2007, Estonia suffered a month long cyber assault to its digital infrastructure, often described as 'Web War I'. In 2010, a worm – Stuxnet – was identified in the supervisory control and data acquisition systems at Iran's uranium enrichment plant, presumably in an attempt to set back Iran's nuclear programme. These illustrations are testament to the reality that dependence upon telecommunications and information infrastructures puts at risk Critical National Infrastructure, and is now at the core of national security interests.

This book takes a detailed look at new theatres of war and considers their relation to international law on the use of force. Except in cases of self-defence or with the authorisation of a Security Council Resolution, the use of force is prohibited under the UN Charter and customary international law. However, the law of *jus ad bellum* was developed in a pre-digital era where current technological capabilities could not be conceived. Jackson Maogoto asks whether the law on the use of force is able to deal with legal disputes likely to arise from modern warfare. Key queries include how one defines an armed attack in an age of anti-satellite weaponry, whether the destruction of a State's vital digital eco-system or the 'blinding' of military communication satellites constitutes a threat, and how one delimits the threshold that would enliven the right of self-defence or retaliatory action. The book argues that while technology has leapt ahead, the legal framework has failed to adapt, rendering States unable to legally defend themselves effectively.

The book will be of interest and use to practitioners, researchers and students of international law generally. Specifically it is of great utility to scholars and practitioners whose interests triangulate use of force, law of armed conflict and the role of established and ascendant technology in these spheres.

Jackson Maogoto is Senior Lecturer at the University of Manchester, UK.

Routledge Research in International Law

Available:

International Law and the Third World
Reshaping Justice
Edited by Richard Falk, Balakrishnan Rajagopal and Jacqueline Stevens

International Legal Theory
Essays and Engagements, 1966–2006
Nicholas Onuf

The Problem of Enforcement in International Law
Countermeasures, the Non-Injured State and the Idea of International Community
Elena Katselli Proukaki

International Economic Actors and Human Rights
Adam McBeth

The Law of Consular Access
A Documentary Guide
John Quigley, William J. Aceves and S. Adele Shank

State Accountability under International Law
Holding States Accountable for a Breach of Jus Cogens Norms
Lisa Yarwood

Technology and the Law on the Use of Force
New Security Challenges in the Twenty-First Century
Jackson Maogoto

Incitement in International Law
Wibke K. Timmermann

International Organizations and the Idea of Autonomy
Institutional Independence in the International Legal Order
Edited by Richard Collins and Nigel D. White

Self-Determination in the Post-9/11 Era
Elizabeth Chadwick

Participants in the International Legal System
Multiple Perspectives on Non-State Actors in International Law
Jean d'Aspremont

Sovereignty and Jurisdiction in the Airspace and Outer Space
Legal Criteria for Spatial Delimitation
Gbenga Oduntan

International Law in a Multipolar World
Edited by Matthew Happold

The Law on the Use of Force
A Feminist Analysis
Gina Heathcote

The ICJ and the Development of International Law
The Lasting Impact of the Corfu Channel Case
Edited by Karine Bannelier, Théodore Christakis and Sarah Heathcote

UNHCR and International Refugee Law
From Treaties to Innovation
Corinne Lewis

Asian Approaches to International Law and the Legacy of Colonialism
The Law of the Sea, Territorial Disputes and International Dispute Settlement
Edited by Jin-Hyun Paik, Seok-Woo Lee, Kevin Y L Tan

The Right to Self-determination Under International Law
'Selfistans,' Secession, and the Rule of the Great Powers
Milena Sterio

Reforming the UN Security Council Membership
The Illusion of Representativeness
Sabine Hassler

Threats of Force
International Law and Strategy
Francis Grimal

The Changing Role of Nationality in International Law
Edited by Alessandra Annoni and Serena Forlati

Criminal Responsibility for the Crime of Aggression
Patrycja Grzebyk

Regional Maintenance of Peace and Security under International Law
The Distorted Mirror
Dace Winther

International Law-Making
Essays in Honour of Jan Klabbers
Edited by Rain Liivoja and Jarna Petman

Resolving Claims to Self-Determination
Is There a Role of the International Court of Justice?
Andrew Coleman

The Rise of Tamil Separatism in Sri Lanka
From Communalism to Secession
Gnanapala Welhengama and Nirmala Pillay

The United Nations and Collective Security
Gary Wilson

Justice for Victims before the International Criminal Court
Luke Moffett

Public-Private Partnerships and Responsibility under International Law
A Global Health Perspective
Lisa Clarke

Cultural Diversity in International Law
The Effectiveness of the UNESCO Convention on the Protection and Promotion of the Diversity of Cultural Expressions
Edited by Lilian Hanania

Forthcoming titles in this series include:

The Cuban Embargo under International Law
El Bloqueo
Nigel D. White

The Changing Nature of Customary International Law
Methods of Interpreting the Concept of Custom in International Criminal Tribunals
Noora Arajärvi

Resisting United Nations Security Council Resolutions
Sufyan Droubi

International Law and Boundary Disputes in Africa
Gbenga Oduntan

Justice in International Law
The Legal, Political, and Moral Dimensions of Indigenous People's Rights
Mauro Barelli

Means of Transportation and Registration of Nationality
Transportation Register by International Organizations
Vincent P. Cogliati-Bantz

The International Criminal Court in Search of its Purpose and Identity
Edited by Triestino Mariniello

Power and Law in International Society
How International Law Influence International Relations
Mark Klamberg

Technology and the Law on the Use of Force

New security challenges in the twenty-first century

Jackson Maogoto

LONDON AND NEW YORK

First published 2015
by Routledge
2 Park Square, Milton Park, Abingdon, Oxon, OX14 4RN

and by Routledge
711 Third Avenue, New York, NY 10017

Routledge is an imprint of the Taylor & Francis Group, an informa business

© 2015 Jackson Maogoto

The right of Jackson Maogoto to be identified as author of this work has been asserted by him in accordance with sections 77 and 78 of the Copyright, Designs and Patents Act 1988.

All rights reserved. No part of this book may be reprinted or reproduced or utilised in any form or by any electronic, mechanical, or other means, now known or hereafter invented, including photocopying and recording, or in any information storage or retrieval system, without permission in writing from the publishers.

Trademark notice: Product or corporate names may be trademarks or registered trademarks, and are used only for identification and explanation without intent to infringe.

British Library Cataloguing in Publication Data
A catalogue record for this book is available from the British Library

Library of Congress Cataloging-in-Publication Data
Maogoto, Jackson Nyamuya, 1975–
  Technology and the law on the use of force: new security challenges in the twenty first century/Jackson Maogoto.
  pages cm – (Routledge research in international law)
  Includes bibliographical references and index.
  ISBN 978-0-415-69433-9 (hardback) – ISBN 978-0-203-71605-2 (ebk) 1. Information warfare (International law) 2. War (International law) 3. Computer networks – Security measures. 4. Cyberterrorism – Prevention. 5. Malware (Computer software) – Prevention. 6. Cyber intelligence (Computer security) 7. Computer security – Law and legislation. I. Title.
  KZ6718.M34 2015
  341.6'3 – dc23
  2014021702

ISBN: 978-0-415-69433-9 (hbk)
ISBN: 978-0-203-71605-2 (ebk)

Typeset in Sabon by
Florence Production Ltd, Stoodleigh, Devon, UK

Contents

Dedication	ix
Acknowledgements	xi
List of acronyms	xiii
Table of cases	xv
Table of statutes	xvii

Introduction   1

1   Use of force: displaced twentieth-century rules, norms and standards?   9

    Introduction 9
    The concept of armed attack 10
    Article 51: the State's right to respond in self-defence 11
        The restrictionist approach 12
        The counter-restrictionist approach 12
    The UN Charter *challenged: shades of legal grey* 13
    The UN Charter: *generalities revisited* 14
    Conclusion 17

2   Revolution in military affairs: hi-tech weaponry, low-tech legal safeguards   23

    Introduction 23
    The fourth domain: outer space 23
    The fifth domain: cyber space 25
    Conclusion 27

3   The fourth domain: ascendance of outer space as a war theatre   31

    Introduction 31
    'Peaceful': easy understanding or difficult enunciation 31

viii *Contents*

    The intersection of the UN Charter *regime on force and Outer Space Law 32*
        Closing the loop? Network centric warfare matures 33
    The Outer Space Treaty *34*
    The Limited Test Ban Treaty *38*
    The Liability Convention *40*
    The Anti-Ballistic Missile Treaty *41*
    Weaponisation and militarisation of outer space revisited 43
    Conclusion 45

4 **War in the fifth domain: cyberwarfare**   53

    Introduction 53
    Cyberattacks: classifications and analytical models 55
        The colours of cyber interruptions and disruptions 56
    Cyber conflict along the spectrum of armed attack 57
        Smokeless warfare: worms, viruses and trojans 58
    Information warfare: colliding or colluding with the regime on the use of force? 59
        Physical destruction: is data property? 60
        Electronic blockades: new perception or old shackles 62
    Small-scale or large-scale attacks: reflections on quantitative evaluation 64
    Specific targeting of military facilities: any difference 65
    Conclusion 67

5 **Discarding law by analogy: old legal frameworks for new threats**   71

    Introduction 71
    Outer space: addressing a clear and present danger 72
        Resolving the 'peaceful purposes' conundrum: disengaging legal shadows from operational substance 72
        Re-orientating the peace and security framework 76
        Coercive arms control 78
        The International Environmental Law Platform 79
    Cyber space: act now not later 83
        Refocusing on the principle of non-intervention 83
        A conclusive multilateral framework? 83
        Rethinking legal thresholds for information warfare 85
    Conclusion 86

Conclusion   91

Bibliography   93
Index   103

Dedication

I wish to thank as always my mother – Mary Salome Gesare Maogoto. She first taught me to read and write. But significantly as I embarked on an academic career she reminded me that teaching is a vocation not a matter of a paycheck at the end of the month. Promise you Mama that I will always work hard and stay dedicated.

To my late father – R. Jackson Nyamuya Maogoto Sr. You were always right and an intellectual. I will never forget your view that the search to know constitutes one of the highest values in society.

To the other main ladies in my life – Helena Anne Anolak (my fiancée). Thanks for being there for me always through thick and thin – you are a gem. To my daughter – Lucija Mary Gesare Maogoto – wonderful was the day you entered our lives. The best ever thing I achieved in life besides my love for my Mama and your mother. Your feistiness is a delight and no doubt I will bear your brunt end for the rest of my life! Be careful, the first thing I am getting rid of as you grow up is my credit cards and cheque book!

To my putative parents-in-law – Chief Greg Anolak and Mrs Osija Anolak. Thank you for believing in me for years and accommodating my imperfections and the nugget of wisdom that I should carve my path in life and not allow dark clouds to shadow my career path. Competence can be a rare commodity

To the late Orion Wenhrynowycz (scholar and gentleman) – the great grandfather of our daughter. Continue to rest in eternal peace. I wish that you would have been around to hold your great granddaughter. However, you live in each one of us. The seeds from your orchard thrive on and you will live eternally on Earth as in heaven.

Acknowledgements

This is the hard part besides labouring on the book as so many individuals were pivotal to this effort. To name all would result in another book length piece!

First, I wish to acknowledge Routledge Publishers for giving me this chance to produce a piece that will end up in their production process. This is quickly followed up by my deep appreciation to Katie Carpenter (Senior Commissioning Editor at Routledge) for her patience and guidance through the early stages of my idea of this monograph. She almost singlehandedly cut through the muddle of my earlier proposal. I hope I have not let down your faith!

Second, I acknowledge Mark Sapwell (Editorial Assistant [Law]) at Routledge. Thank you for your patience and tolerance as well as enthusiasm and cheer that made a daunting task much easier.

Third, I wish to express my gratitude to the British Institute of International and Comparative Law (BIICL) for the privilege of spending my six-month sabbatical with them in 2012. The vibrant intellectual environment was a core aspect as I wrestled to firm out and streamline the research on this work. Professor Robert McCorquodale (Director of the Institute) made sure that I was kept on my toes from time to time during group gatherings. I would bolt to the library if I was caught short to firm out my research – thank you. To Geoffrey Sautner (the BIICL Office Manager) – I now know where the coffee machine is, the computer terminals and the Institute's library, but most importantly your all round support and care for all Visiting Scholars and Fellows.

Last and by no means least I wish to thank the Godparents of my daughter – Eric Halidou and Kristi Maksimik – you support me in more ways than you realise. Finally, Commander Timothy Robinson and Mrs Ania Robinson – all I can say is thank you.

Acronyms

ABM	Anti-Ballistic Missile
ABM Treaty	*Treaty on the Limitation of Anti-Ballistic Missile Systems*
ARAMCO	Saudi Arabian Oil Company
ASAT	Anti-Satellite Weapon
CD	Conference on Disarmament
CNA	Computer Network Attack
CNE	Computer Network Exploitation
CNI	Critical National Infrastructure
COPUOS	Committee on the Peaceful Uses of Outer Space
CPNI	Centre for the Protection of National Infrastructures
DDoS	Distributed Denial of Service
DoD	US Department of Defence
DEW	Direct Energy Weapons
E-Bomb	Electromagnetic Pulse Bombs
EMP	Electromagnetic Pulse
GEO	geo-synchronous orbit
GIG	Global Information Grid
GPS	Global Positioning System
HPM	High-powered Microwaves
ICBM	Inter-Continental Ballistic Missile
ICJ	International Court of Justice
ITC	*International Telecommunications Convention*
IW	Information Warfare
LEO	low-Earth orbit
Liability Convention	*Liability Convention on Damage Caused by Space Objects*
MAD	Mutual Assured Destruction
malware	Malicious Software
Maser	Microwave Amplification by Stimulated Emission of Radiation
MoD	Ministry of Defence

NATO CCD COE	NATO Cooperative Cyber Defence Centre of Excellence
NAVSTAR	Navigation Satellite Timing and Ranging
NFIRE	Near Field Infrared Experiment
NATO	North Atlantic Treaty Organisation
OOTW	Operations Other than War
PLC	Programmable Logic Controllers
RMA	Revolution in Military Affairs
SCADA	Supervisory Control and Data Acquisition
SDI	Strategic Defense Initiative
SSO	sun-synchronous orbit
Tallinn Manual	*Tallinn Manual on the International Law Applicable to Cyber Warfare*
TCA	Transformational Communication Architecture
UK	United Kingdom
UN	United Nations
UN Charter	*Charter of the United Nations*
US	United States of America
USAF	United States Air Force
US-CCU	United States Cyber-Consequences Unit
USSPACECOM	United States Space Command
USSR	Union of Soviet Socialist Republics (Soviet Union)
WMD	Weapons of Mass Destruction

Table of cases

Advisory Opinion on the Legality of the Threat or Use of Nuclear
    Weapons (1996) 226, ICJ 40, 50n
Military and Paramilitary Activities In and Against Nicaragua
    (Nicaragua *v*. US 1986, ICJ (June 27) 1111 2345) 18n, 65, 67, 83

Table of statutes

Anti-Ballistic Missile (ABM) Treaty
    (1972) 41–43, 51n
    Art. I 42, 51n
    Art. II 42
    Art. II(1) 51n
    Art. III 42
    Art. V 42
    Art. V(1) 51n, 52n
    Art. XII 42
    Art. XII(1)–(2) 51n

Biological Weapons Conventions
    (1972) 92n

Charter of the United Nations
    (UN Charter)
    Art. 1 78
    Art. 2(3) 59
    Art. 2(4) 10, 12, 13, 18n,
                    44, 55, 59, 62, 63,
                    64, 65, 72, 86
    Art. 39 .... 59, 78
    Art. 41 63
    Art. 42 63
    Art. 44 10
    Art. 51 .... 10–13, 35, 40,
                    58, 59, 64, 86
    Preamble 10–11
        para. 7 10
Convention on International
    Liability for Damage
    Caused by Space Objects
    (Liability Convention)
    1972 40–41
    Art. I(b) 50n
    Art. III 51n

Art. IX 40
Convention on Registration of
    Objects Launched into Outer
    Space (Registration
    Convention) 1974
    Art. II 82
    Art. II(1) 82, 88n
    Art. VI 82, 88n

Gas Protocol (1925) 92n

International Telecommunications
    Convention (ITC)
    Art. .... 12(2)(f) 84
    Art. .... 12(4) 84

Liability Convention see Convention
    on International Liability for
    Damage Caused by Space
    Objects (Liability Convention)
    1972
Limited Test Ban Treaty see Treaty
    Banning Nuclear Weapon
    Tests in the Atmosphere,
    in Outer Space and Under
    Water (Limited Test Ban
    Treaty) 1963

Outer Space Treaty see Treaty on
    Principles Governing the
    Activities of States in the
    Exploration and Use of
    Outer Space, including the
    Moon and Other Celestial
    Bodies (Outer Space Treaty)
    1967

Treaty Banning Nuclear Weapon Tests in the Atmosphere, in Outer Space and Under Water (Limited Test Ban Treaty) 1963 ... 38–40, 47n, 50n
   Art. I 39, 49n
   Art. I(1) 39–40
   Art. I(1)(b) 49n
   Preamble 38–39, 50n
Treaty Between the United States of America and the Union of Soviet Socialist Republics on the Limitation of Anti-Ballistic Missile Systems *see* Anti-Ballistic Missile (ABM) Treaty (1972)
Treaty on Principles Governing the Activities of States in the Exploration and Use of Outer Space, including the Moon and Other Celestial Bodies (Outer Space Treaty) 1967 .... 47n, 72, 75
   Art. I 35, 48n
   Art. II 35, 48n
   Art. III 35, 48n, 73
   Art. IV 35–37, 38, 48n, 81–82
   Art. IV(1) 37, 38, 48n
   Art. IV(2) 37, 48n, 51n
   Art. VI 82
   Art. VII 82, 88n

UN Charter *see* Charter of the United Nations

Vienna Convention on the Law of Treaties (1969) 73, 86n

Introduction

Physical destruction through use of soldiers, guns and bombs is the primary basis of modern military conflict. The turn of the twentieth century saw the maturation of the nation-at-arms in which war was waged across an entire nation in a bid to not only decimate a protagonist's soldiers but also to degrade its infrastructure and thus weaken its war fighting capability. Attenuating war fighting capability encompasses degrading an opponent's transport, communication and industrial capacity. World War I is an exemplar – and large-scale wars since. Progressively as technology became essential to society the number of targets also increased.

The 1950s saw the conquering of outer space after technological and engineering breakthroughs resulted in the placing of satellites in outer space. This marked a giant leap for mankind in science and communications and subsequently a new platform with military utility. It was the same era that saw the initial development of computers, which in a few short decades would lead to the maturation of the Internet – anchored primarily by space assets. In time, the synergy of outer space and the Internet was to place information firmly at the forefront of methods and means of 'smart warfare' – essentially the integration of military assets into battle platforms.

By the 1990s, the Internet, which began as a military experiment in the mid-1960s, had revolutionised communication networks and infrastructure and is now entrenched in society.[1] Its widespread use and dependence in contemporary times has simultaneously generated different spectrums of use and management of infrastructure, risk and liability.[2] Critical National Infrastructure (CNI), such as banking and finance, electric power, telecommunications and transportation, is now dependent upon the information systems and processes and thus very susceptible to disruption or disablement through hostile satellite and internet intrusions. The twenty-first century has also witnessed the maturation of the progressive shift that had been underway for several decades towards a reliance on information as a force multiplier in harnessing military kinetic capabilities. The concrete precursor of the ascendant Revolution in Military Affairs (RMA) underpinned by information technology was manifest in the military technology displayed by coalition forces during the first Gulf War in 1991 through the use of 'smart' precision-guided kinetic weapons.[3]

In the twenty-first century, threats to governmental, economic and military interests via the information infrastructure are multiplying exponentially with governments heavily dependent and increasingly so on information infrastructure.[4] With governmental and non-governmental operations supported by vast automated systems and electronic data, 'the risks are very high and the breadth of potential impact very wide'.[5] Information frameworks and assets are now central as physical and virtual technological processes now undergird fundamental value-added capabilities of traditional infrastructure, which were and still are premised on tangibility.[6] In 2001, a US Congressional Research Service (CRS) Report highlighted the pervasiveness and seriousness of threats to digital ecosystems, noting that the risk of cyber warfare presents an emerging area of national interest, which in turn meant it was a significant threat to national security.[7] The observation was prescient. Six years later, alleged Chinese hackers disabled hundreds of US Department of Defence (DoD) computers.[8] In the same year, cyber attacks strongly linked to Russia crippled the Estonian government and commercial computer networks.[9] The following year, Georgia witnessed attacks on its digital ecosystem prior to and in the course of a short war with Russia. The identity of the perpetrators in the planning and execution of the attacks remained only strongly circumstantial as the Russian government strongly and formally denied any role.

As the twenty-first century progresses, the 'information' RMA, which encompasses technologies that 'gather, process and fuse information on a large geographical area in real time, all the time'[10], is now a dominant feature of military planning and operations. Information RMA now encompasses the application of communication technology to the military arena and is a crucial nexus in the integration of sea-based, air-based and land-based resources into one battleground platform. The connector is the use of sophisticated communication, reconnaissance and real-time information technologies. This is now central to the planning and execution of military operations as a force multiplier that aids preservation of military superiority and advantage across a broad variety of military operations.[11] Strategic assets are no longer the number of guns and planes a State possesses, but also significantly its ability to integrate electronic weapon systems. Essentially, information networks are central to force multiplication. Today, the mass or metrics of military hardware depend on the ability of a State to use information precisely to elicit more effective outcomes underpinned as well by the Internet's open architecture and suitability in waging asymmetrical warfare.[12] This lies behind the sustained efforts by States (major and medium military powers) in developing Computer Network Attack (CNA) capacity.[13] By way of illustration, a couple of examples are proffered at this stage but as the book progresses more detailed and broader initiatives by States will be articulated. In 2011, India (an ascendant military power) noted that cyber security entails 'protecting information and information systems (networks, computers, data bases, data centers and applications'.[14] It went on to note that cyber defence encompassed activities 'primarily originating from hostile actors that have political, quasi political or economic motivation' impacting on 'national security, public safety or well-being of society'.[15] A year later, the UK (an established military power) noted in its *Cyber Security Strategy* Report that it would 'expand the Centre for the Protection of National Infrastructure's (CPNI) provision of bilateral cyber risk advice to reach more private companies of importance to the UK'.[16] This brief snapshot of positions reflects the seriousness to national security posed by threats to CNI by a cross-section of States since militaries are also in large measure, dependent upon the civilian information infrastructure.[17] Vast spectra of military information infrastructures are now in differing degrees either dependent on, or integrated with, civilian information infrastructure over which governments have little control and thus multiplying vulnerability to attacks. Robert Anderson and P.M. Feldman note:

> [T]he linkage between information systems and traditional critical infrastructures has increased the scope and potential of the information warfare threat... This in turn creates a tunnel of vulnerability previously unrealized in the history of conflict.[18]

The spectra of vulnerability essentially means that operational aspects of offensive and defensive actions in the military arena cover actions that may be tantamount to hostile acts or demonstration of hostile intent. Many actions can and do fall below the traditional threshold under the regime on the use of force. This means they trigger a 'response crisis' by creating legal confusion relating to which forms of force deployment to use and rules of engagement to base on among other indicia doctrines on imminence and proportionality.[19] Access, denial or degradation to information networks complicates the battlefield by posing a confusing mixture of actions by statal and non-statal actions. It is on this basis that information operations are destabilising the existing global State system upon which traditional rules of armed conflict have rested for decades in light of the complexity and flexibility of new non-kinetic intrusions.

New forms of 'virtual' weaponry and changing international re-conceptualisations of sovereignty and territory brought about by global interdependence by boundless boundaries have solidified the reality that outer and cyber spaces as digital commons have outstripped extant regulatory frameworks. The peculiarity and challenge of these global commons is that they tend to defy and cut across standard boundaries/jurisdictions and distinctions between war and peace, civilian and military responses and ultimately legal and illegal. This means that events or activities in outer and cyber spaces cause legal consequences, which are often not captured in the bright line distinctions of classical statist defined military applications and processes. Dependence upon telecommunications and information infrastructures puts at risk economic, political and military security making the defence of CNI one of the cores of national security interests. The basis in practical terms is relatively simple; information is now central to conflict as a primary conduit.

Force projection through technology as noted is underpinned by space assets. In this regard, it is important to note that in the twenty-first century the focus has been almost on a singular fixation with the Internet and cyber threats pushing outer space into the periphery of mainstream discussion. Yet it is outer space assets that form the backbone of information operations and has over several decades been the basis of the various evolutionary phases of the information RMA, subsequently multiplied by the maturation of the Internet. It is the dozens of civilian and military satellites circling in orbit night and day that form the pivots of terrestrial and non-terrestrial information networks. Space assets essentially undergird a State's ability to co-ordinate and maintain integrated battleground platforms including command and control strategic capacity. As the book unfolds, the general premise is outer space as the fourth domain in warfare with cyber space as the fifth domain (after the traditional spheres of land, air and sea). Thus one of the book's central themes of discussion is to address these two information platforms and *in particular* reiterate the importance of outer space assets as an integral component of the information RMA.

In the context of information warfare activities between States, the use of force regime embodied in the *Charter of the United Nations* (*UN Charter*)[20] leaves room for ambiguities. This is mainly because its focus at founding was kinetic force (physical destruction) and not non-kinetic force (electronic intrusions). It may be averred that the regime on the use of force is flexible and it can cover outer space militarisation and weaponisation as well as cyber warfare. It is to be noted here that militarisation and weaponisation of outer space has convergences and divergences. Militarisation of outer space has been around for decades since satellites were launched.[21] Weaponisation of outer space refers to the placement in orbit of space-based devices that have a destructive capacity.[22]

The argument that conflict and the basis of sovereign States and the reality of global digital networks can find accommodation within the extant regime on the use of force is not straightforward. For example and significantly, any attempt to analogise outer and cyber spaces to the other global common – the High Seas regime – potentially misses the point that the High Seas regime is premised on geographical parameters and does not necessarily have the same dynamics as the digital global commons, owing to the reality that operationally a bulk of their operation and processes regularly occur through boundless boundaries.

In the twenty-first century, the world finds itself back in a Cold War paradigm with the world's military powers increasingly reliant for their

Introduction   5

military mobilisation and security on space assets and information networks. Billions of dollars are and continue to be spent by States on defensive systems apprehensive of new security threats in a digital world increasingly posed by the dynamics of outer and cyber space. The conundrum is aptly summed up by Timothy Coughlin's observation that:

> The dichotomy between law and technology has long been tenuous in the best of times, and irreconcilable at the worst. Answering to different masters, technological development and legal structures are in a constant state of ebb and flow, with each pushing the contours of the other in a choreographed exchange of concessions and compromises.[23]

This book tackles broad themes but confines itself to two spectra. First, it focuses only on those information intrusions that are instigated by or imputable to States and not the activities of non-State actors acting outside the realm of links to State activity (generally or specifically), as non-statal activity generally falls within the spectrum of national or transnational criminality rather than the use of force paradigm. Second, it constrains itself by focusing on aspects of *jus ad bellum* rather than *jus in bello*. The caveat is that admittedly there are no bright line distinctions in operation as the law would have it and thus from time to time references may be made to *jus in bello*. However, by and large the book seeks to avoid the pitfalls of conflating these two aspects wholesale but occasionally may. It is hoped that it succeeds in this intricate and complex endeavour more than it fails in seeking to wield together what parallels of outer and cyber spaces and convergences rather than divergences. Often these spaces are discussed in mainstream literature from one perspective or the other.

The reference from time to time to digital ecosystems is broadly used to cover the multi-layered aspects of information and electronic uses through the various platforms of outer and cyber spaces. It is to be noted that various definitions cover different aspects meaning they are largely terms of arts. The interchangeable use of terms is not to create or signal an appearance of confusion but rather the reality that there are no distinct common and settled scientific meanings. Different authors and commentators often use different designations. To seek to synchronise this would effectively be to impose a different terminology to the works in question. For clarity, a full list of acronyms is provided at the start of the book.

Chapter 1 introduces the use of force regime underpinned by the *UN Charter* and its dictates. While the *UN Charter* remains the dominant reference point there has always been debate on its full ambit – waxing and waning with episodic State practice. This chapter will examine the broad vista of the use of force regime with a particular focus on the aspects linked or bearing on extant and emergent challenges posed by the information RMA. The precise parameters of what constitutes the use of force are well-defined – conventional kinetic weapons attacks are included within the *UN Charter*. Extrapolating, outer space and cyber-based intrusions intended to cause physical damage to tangible property or injury or death to human beings may reasonably be included, but it is on this point that some crucial issues arise. Can non-kinetic acts through outer or cyber spaces trigger an international response based on the definition of use of force? Thus Chapter 1 focuses on primary aspects of the extant regime on the use of force. The seeming general sketch is not so much to be simplistic, but because the doctrines and principles identified are subsequently contextualised in the discussions on outer and cyber space activities in Chapters 3 and 4.

Chapter 2 focuses on the information RMA and the problems that military technology in the twenty-first century poses. Space and cyber attacks may not destroy life or property but can degrade it through a variety of means involving electronic and digital incursions and interference. Technology noted briefly in this introduction has advanced to the point where military forces now have the capability to inflict injury, death and destruction across time and space with attacks ranging from relatively innocuous infiltration of State information networks to attacks (benign or severe) on CNI. While conventional kinetic methods of warfare fit comfortably within traditional use of force analysis and some non-kinetic uses, lower-level attacks present a problem as they often cross the distinction between acts of force and acts of intrusion.

Chapter 3 introduces and discusses outer space as a crucial component in information RMA. This chapter is geared to disaggregate the mostly singular focus by scholars and commentators on cyber warfare that seems to have displaced space assets as the backbone of information RMA and the reality that space assets are glued to cyber capabilities. States have for years been undertaking what might be termed 'passive' military activities in outer space. Currently, outer space assets are even more critical in military activities threading in cyber uses.

Chapter 4 focuses on cyber space. Computerised weapons systems and wired infantry have blown away some of the fog of war from the battlefield, but covered cyber space in a thick blanket of legal and policy uncertainty. Several militaries now possess specialised cyber units whose functions and mandate include defending digitised ecosystems that extend to compromising those of third parties. Questions permeate including: What are to be the new strategic concepts as States invest ever increasing funds in defensive and offensive cyber weapons? What would be the threshold regarding the identity of an attacker? What should be the threshold to trigger a response?

Chapter 5 rounds up with reflections and evaluations on how extant international law principles and discourse offer a framework to constrain hostile actions in outer and cyber spaces. This pointed reflection seeks to identify aspects of the digital commons that fall within existing legal principles and doctrines in addressing emerging and ascendant aspects of the militarisation and weaponisation of the digital global commons.

Notes

1. See e.g. Wilske, S. and Schiller, T. (1997) 'International Jurisdiction in Cyberspace: Which States May Regulate the Internet', *Federal Communications Law Journal*, 50: 117, 119.
2. See e.g. The Report of the President's Commission on Critical Infrastructure Protection (1997) *Critical Foundations: Protecting America's Infrastructure*, 16–17, [online] available at www.ciao.gov/PCCIP/PCCIP_Report.pdf (accessed 21 December 2013).
3. See e.g. Kiernan, V. (1991) 'War Tests Satellites' Prowess, Military Space Systems Put to Work during Desert Storm Conflict'. *Space News*, 21 January; Meyer, J.J. (1993) 'Communications: The Way Ahead', *Military Law Review*, 43(3): 85.
4. See e.g. Andrews, D.P. (1996) *Report of the Defense Science Board Task Force on Information Warfare Defense*. Washington, DC: Office of the Secretary of Defense; Bowers, D.C. (1998) 'Information Warfare: The Computer Revolution is Altering How Future Wars will be Conducted', *Armed Forces Journal International*, 38–9.
5. Burnell, Scott (2001) 'US Computer Security Called Inadequate' *United Press International* (27 September), [online] available at www.upi.com/Science_News/2001/09/26/US-computer-security-called-inadequate/UPI-36121001543964/ (accessed 31 July 2014).
6. For example, see Romero, P.M. (2006) 'An Immunological Approach to Counter-Terrorism and Infrastructure Defense Law in Electronic Domains', *International Journal of Law and Information Technology*, 101, 104. While Philip Romero makes this observation in regard to Western societies, the reality is that now it is true of every State as automation becomes critical to all including Third World countries.
7. See e.g. Hildreth, S. (2001) *Congressional Research Service (CRS) Report for Congress, 'Cyberwarfare'* 15, [online] available at http://fas.org/irp/crs/RL30735.pdf (accessed 12 October 2012).
8. See e.g. Hosenball, M. (2007) 'Whacking Hackers', *Newsweek*. 15 October, 10.
9. See e.g. Landler, M. and Markoff, J. 'After Computer Siege on Estonia, War Fears Turn to Cyberspace'. *New York Times*, 29 May, A1.
10. Owens, W.A. (1995–96) 'The American Revolution in Military Affairs', *Joint Force Quarterly*, 37.
11. See e.g. Gompert, D.C. and Lachow, I. (2000) 'Transforming US Forces: Lessons from a Wider Revolution', *Rand Issue Paper*, 193, [online] available at www.rand.org/publications/IP/IP193/ (accessed 18 February 2012); Bartlett, H.C. (1996) 'Force Planning, Military Revolutions and the Tyranny of Technology'. *Strategic Review*, 24(4): 28–40 (Fall).
12. See e.g. Wingfield, T. (2000) *The Law of Information Conflict, National Security Law in Cyberspace*. Huntsville, AL: Aegis Research Corporation, 21.
13. See e.g. Wilson, C. 'Information Operations, Electronic Warfare, and Cyberwar: Capabilities and Related Policy'. Issues 5 *Congressional Research Services (CRS) Report for Congress Order Code RL31787*, [online] available at www.fas.org.library.newcastle.edu.au/sgp/crs/natsec/RL31787.pdf (accessed 12 October 2012).
14. Department of Information Technology (2011) 'Ministry of Communications and Information Technology, Government of India: Discussion draft on National Cyber Security', 5, [online] available at http://deity.gov.in/content/discussion-draft-national-cyber-security-policy (accessed 15 April 2011).
15. Ibid.

8 *Introduction*

16 Cabinet Office (2012) 'The UK Cyber Security Strategy: Report on Progress', December 2012, Forward Plans', 2. available at www.gov.uk/government/uploads/system/uploads/attachment_data/file/265402/Cyber_Security_Strategy_Forward_Plans_3-Dec-12_1.pdf (accessed 5 August 2013).
17 See e.g. Andrews, D.P. (1996) *Report of the Defense Science Board Task Force on Information Warfare Defense*, Washington, DC: Office of the Secretary of Defense.
18 Anderson, R.H. and Feldman, P.M. (1999) *Securing the US Defense Information Infrastructure: A Proposed Approach*. Santa Monica, CA: RAND.
19 See O'Donnell, B.T. and Kraska, J.C. (2002) 'Humanitarian Law: Developing International Rules for the Digital Battlefield', *Journal of Conflict and Security Law*, 133, 148.
20 *UN Charter*, 26 June 1945, 59 Stat. 1031, 892 UNTS 119.
21 Militaries rely on satellites for command and control, communication, monitoring, early warning and navigation with the Global Positioning Systems (GPS).
22 Under certain circumstances, ground-based systems designed or used to attack space-based assets also constitute space weapons.
23 Coughlin, T. (2011) 'The Future of Robotic Weaponry and the Law of Armed Conflict: Irreconcilable Differences?', *UCL Jurisprudence Review*, 67–8.

1 Use of force

Displaced twentieth-century rules, norms and standards?

Introduction

In the twenty-first century, military powers are concentrating on projecting military power through incorporation of technology geared toward leaner and efficient projections of force. As the evolution of outer and cyber spaces into distinct theatres of military operations unfolds, a serious legal deficit is exposed in the absence of specific or tangential international norms restricting the use of means and methods of war in these digital commons. The regime on Outer Space Law is not necessarily patchy with regard to militarisation and weaponisation. However, key provisions of relevant treaties and instruments have been overtaken by the tremendous technological and engineering breakthroughs, particularly in the course of the last four decades of the twentieth century. On one hand the provisions of key instruments offer broad interpretational leeway for and against the militarisation and weaponisation of outer space, while on the other hand, cyber warfare itself sits uneasily within the *UN Charter* regime on the use of force. This is in light of the *UN Charter* drafters' almost singular fixation on conventional land, air and sea warfare – essentially kinetic (physical destruction) force. Thus it is notable that:

> An armed attack involves the use of armed force and not mere economic damage. Economic damage, for example, by way of trade suspension, or by use of a computer virus designed to paralyse the financial operations of a State's stock exchange or to disable the technology ... may have a devastating impact on the victim State but the principles governing the right to use force in self-defence are confined to a *military* attack.[1]

Turning back to the *UN Charter* in light of the quote above, when it was drafted in 1945, the right of self-defence was the only included exception (reserved to State discretion) to the general prohibition of the use of force. Under the *UN Charter*, unilateral acts of force regardless of motive were made illegal. Individual or collective self-defence became the cornerstone relating to use of force and since then has been invoked with regard to almost every use of external military force.

The pivot on which present day *jus ad bellum* hinges is firstly on Article 2(4) of the *Charter*, which articulates the principle of the prohibition of force in international relations.[2] This provision introduced to international politics a radically new notion: a general prohibition of the unilateral resort to force by States. The Article asserts the need for peaceful resolution of disputes stating that: 'All members shall refrain in their international relations from the threat or use of force against the territorial integrity or political independence of any State, or in any other manner inconsistent with the purposes of the UN.'[3] The terms 'territorial integrity' and 'political independence' are not intended to restrict the scope of the prohibition of the use of force. Rather, the two indicia cover any possible kind of transboundary use of armed force.[4]

The next section of this chapter will outline generalities of the *UN Charter* on the concepts and principles that undergird the thresholds relating to the use of force. As stated in the Introduction of this book, this chapter is specifically geared to be an outline rather than a detailed overview premised on the book's themes. Based on this, it will flag issues that are germane to the book's analysis and should not be perceived as a merely simplistic and parochial enunciation of the complexities relating to the extant use of force regime.

The concept of armed attack

Paragraph 7 of the Preamble to the *UN Charter* states that one of the core goals of the UN is 'that armed force shall not be used, save in the common interest'. Article 44 reinforces this view. The *Charter* uses the term 'force' alluding to the fact that in light of the *travaux preparatoires* only military force was at that time in history the concern of the prohibition of the use of force.[5] This conclusion is confirmed by the *Declaration of Friendly Relations* adopted by the UN General Assembly on 24 October 1970.[6] In interpreting the principle that States shall refrain in their international relations from the threat or use of force, the Declaration deals solely with military force.[7] This prescription means military force is premised on conventional means – essentially kinetic force. As Gerry Simpson notes:

> Traditionally, the concept of an 'armed attack' was understood to involve a cross-border use of military force by one State against another ... In other words, the *UN Charter* was designed to prevent or forestall or confront a repeat of the last war, the Second World War. This may account for its lack of precision and guidance in relation to unconventional uses of force since then.[8]

Mathew Waxman bolsters Simpson's view, averring that

> the *Charter*'s preamble sets out the goal that '*armed* force ... not be used save in the common interest.' ... Article 51 speaks of self-defense

against 'armed' attacks. There are textual counter-arguments, such as that Article 51's more specific limit to 'armed attacks' suggests that drafters envisioned prohibited 'force' as a broader category not limited to particular methods. However, the discussions of means throughout the *Charter* and the document's negotiating history strongly suggest the drafters' intention to regulate armed force differently and more strictly than other coercive instruments.[9]

Essentially then the framework for analysing armed attacks is traditionally relatively well settled including the core legal principles governing its meaning. Accompanying armed attacks are the indicia of scope, duration and intensity in evaluating whether a particular use of force constitutes an armed attack.[10] Harkening back to the French language version of the *UN Charter*, it refers to 'armed aggression' rather than an 'armed attack'. About three decades after the *UN Charter* entered into force, in 1974, the UN General Assembly passed a resolution on the *Definition of Aggression*.[11] The resolution requires an attack to be of 'sufficient gravity' before it is considered an armed attack.[12] While the resolution never defines armed attacks, it provides examples that are widely accepted by the international community.[13] It is to be noted that the resolution primarily deals with conventional attacks. While the resolution helped settle the meaning of armed attacks for conventional attacks, the more technology has advanced, the more attacks have come in forms not previously covered by various State declarations and practices.[14]

Article 51: the State's right to respond in self-defence

The *UN Charter* permits State actions that are reasonably necessary in self-defence when faced with an 'armed attack'.[15] Article 51 provides that '[n]othing in the present *Charter* shall impair the inherent right of individual or collective self-defence . . .'.[16] This defensive right exists until the Security Council mobilises to halt the attack. The term 'armed attack' represents the key notion of the concept of self-defence pursuant to Article 51. In the final analysis, its interpretation determines how far unilateral force is still admissible.

As straightforward as Article 51 appears, its interpretation and application remains a source of considerable debate in much the same way as the concepts of 'armed attack' and 'use or threat of force'. The key difficulty in interpreting Article 51 is the word 'inherent'. While the *UN Charter* does not indicate what rights are 'inherent', the inclusion of this term was considered significant by the drafters of the *Charter*. The initial draft of Article 51 made no mention of this 'inherent right', but it was changed to make the definition of self-defence acknowledge that right.[17] Two schools of thought have developed with regard to the scope of Article 51 – those who take the restrictive (literal) approach and those who take the counter-restrictive (expansive) view. Depending on which position one takes, self-defence may be viewed either as solely predicated on a responsive act to a current attack or as a broader notion encompassing in certain circumstances anticipatory acts to an imminent threat of attack.

The restrictionist approach

Restrictionists adhere to the argument that the term 'inherent right' doesn't modify self-defence in any meaningful way, meaning the requirement of some incursion beyond national borders must occur before the right is activated.[18] The restrictionist approach cites the absolute prohibition of resort to forcible self-help as set out in Article 2(4) subject only to the limited exception contained in Article 51, which permits recourse to self-defence only when faced with an actual 'armed attack'. The Article does not contemplate anticipatory or pre-emptive actions by a State that is merely threatened or apprehensive of hostile acts by a Third State. Rather, it requires a State to refrain from responding with force unless actively engaged in repelling an armed attack.[19] If the correctness of the view is that Article 51 of the *UN Charter* is the authoritative definition of the right of self-defence and is not qualified or supplemented by the customary law and is accepted, then States are bound by the black-letter law of the *Charter*. Under this understanding, States have less extensive grounds to support armed force undertaken other than within the framework of the *UN Charter*.[20] This reinforces Article 2(4)'s prohibition on the use of force and the complementary Article 51 right of self-defense within the ambit of military attacks or armed violence.'[21] As a follow on, and to flag an aspect that will be discussed, Michael Waxman (2011) notes that:

> [r]eading Article 2(4)'s prohibition of force to include such intrusion into another sovereign's domain would lead to the conclusion that ... like past efforts to define Article 2(4) 'force' as coercion, efforts to expand its coverage beyond armed force so as to include violations of sovereign domain such as propaganda or political subversion never gained significant traction.[22]

The counter-restrictionist approach

The counter-restrictionist approach adopts an expansionist view. Proponents interpret the word 'inherent' to mean that the *UN Charter* recognises and includes those rights of self-defence that existed under customary international law prior to the drafting of the *Charter*.[23] The counter-restrictionists argue that 'inherent right' is used to preserve the meaning of 'self-defence' as it existed prior to the founding of the UN. The argument is premised on the fact that under customary international law, the right of self-defence should also be judged by the standard first set out in the 1837 incident of

The Caroline.[24] This established the right of a State to take necessary and proportional actions in anticipation of a hostile threat.[25] Proponents have often (and particularly in recent years) cited the impracticability of applying a literal interpretation of Article 51 in an age of advanced weapons and delivery systems and heightened trans-national terrorist activity throughout the world. The fulcrum of this stance is that self-defence actions may be taken in anticipation of a given threat and as an immediate response to actions directed at the vital interests of the target State.[26]

Michael Byers explains that customary law traditionally recognises a limited right of pre-emptive self-defence according to the *Caroline* criteria – 'a necessity of self-defence, instant, overwhelming, leaving no choice of means and no moment for deliberation' precipitating action that is not 'unreasonable or excessive'.[27] In support, Martti Koskenniemi notes that the right of self-defence articulated in the *UN Charter* 'should be read rationally against the useful purpose the rule is intended to serve'[28] noting that the purpose of Article 51 is 'to protect the sovereignty and independence of the State'.[29] This raises the spectre that a State that feels its sovereignty and independence to be threatened by the actions of another country might be entitled to use force against that State even if the hostile actions may not have risen to the level of an actual armed attack based on the indicia of scope, duration and intensity. Malcolm Shaw notes that . . . 'the notion of armed attack within the context of justifying recourse to force in self-defence should be understood as including actions which contribute significantly to the attack itself . . .'.[30] In the past and often from time to time there has been discourse waxing and waning over time that:

> Article 2(4) reads its purpose more expansively and looks not at the instrument used but its general effect: that it prohibits coercion. Armed force is only one instrument of coercion, and the easiest to identify. This interpretation of Article 2(4) stresses its purpose over its text.[31]

The *UN Charter* challenged: shades of legal grey

Traditionally, the factors at play in determining whether an act is a use of force (as noted above) are relatively straightforward requiring the use of weaponry that produce kinetic impact (some type of explosion or physical force). Thus, what constitutes the parameters on use of force is largely clear. Conventional weapon attacks are included in Article 2(4) considering that despite attempts by some States to include threats of force and economic coercion within Article 2(4) during the drafting of the *UN Charter* the majority of the States effectively resisted this viewpoint.[32] However, as technology advances analysis has gone beyond kinetic impact towards a result-oriented approach in which destruction of life or property is embraced. For example, it this dynamic that sees chemical and biological weaponry encompassed within the ambit of the use of force. The advent of technological and engineering breakthroughs just like nuclear weapons has added novelty and created difficult legal and political questions that burden the doctrine of self-defence. These developments radically change the role that threats of warfare now play in its applications to the fourth and fifth domains regarding military related activities and ultimately warfare.

Due to new ascendant (non-kinetic) means and methods of warfare, a legal consensus has yet to congeal on what constitutes a hostile case of real or potential intrusion that could trigger reaction by a target State. A significant part of the issue lies in the various perspectives that can and cannot qualify as an act of war within the confines of the *UN Charter* definition of a 'use of force'.[33] First, the interference of outer space assets or computer networks that do not generate physical destruction do not involve the use of 'force' as traditionally defined when no physical damage is caused. Second is the matter of the legal threshold of attributing an attack, for example the jamming of a satellite or computer network or process. Those responsible for the attack have to be ascertained by establishing a sufficient nexus between the origin and the perpetrator. In matters of satellite interference as subsequently discussed in Chapter 3, it is relatively more straightforward when physical means are used such as ground based lasers or the more familiar classic kinetic based weapon – say an Anti-Satellite Weapon (ASAT) weapon. However, the matter may not be as straightforward when 'rogue' computer programming shifts another State's satellite into a collisional orbital path.

The *UN Charter*: generalities revisited

Military blueprints by military powers now encapsulate concepts of space support and cyber enhancement alluding to the central role of information and technology in facilitating military operations. The accelerating pace towards accommodating outer and cyber space attacks through formation of dedicated unites and incorporation in military doctrines poses difficult legal questions by presenting new forms of danger to international peace and security. While for almost its entire history, the UN in general, and the Security Council in particular, have approached their mission in a reactive manner; this stance is increasing untenable in the face of new threats specifically here – a determined push by leading military powers to not only dominate but also to control outer and cyber spaces with military intent underpinning the more traditional national security considerations. The applicable legal principles beg the question of whether the extant international use of force regime encapsulates advances in use and deployment of technology in military planning and operations.

The prospect of space warfare points to a military paradigm premised on 'counterforce', which in and of itself implicitly encompasses pre-emptive or retaliatory strikes. A broad right of anticipatory self-defence premised on a standard of 'emerging threat' would introduce dangerous uncertainties relating to the determination of potential threats justifying pre-emptive action. What comes to the fore is how militarisation of the two digital commons reveals deficiencies in current international law. For instance, in 2003 the Chinese People's Daily quoted a Chinese military strategist as saying: 'In the current and future State security strategy, if one wants not to be controlled by others, one must have considerable space scientific and technological strength.'[34] Later, a Chinese military official commented that China's army had already introduced the concept of 'space force strength'[35] in apparent reference to a similar US military concept. The official went on to note that a Chinese military research report proposed building a separate 'force to fight in space'.

In the spectrum of cyber space, information networks' legal definitions of armed attack and self-defence as articulated in the *UN Charter* form (even in the twenty-first century) the norms for contemporary State behaviour in use of force parameters. Claims that a foreign government has surreptitiously penetrated another country's information infrastructure and caused actual physical harm raises complex factual issues not previously present when States confronted and attacked each another through armies, planes, ships, tanks and artillery.[36] In a testimony before the US Congress in 2000, John Serabian Jr – an intelligence expert – testified to the growing threats from foreign nations in the cyber space domain poignantly noting:

> We are detecting, with increasing frequency, the appearance of doctrine and dedicated offensive cyber-warfare programs in other countries. We have identified several ... government-sponsored offensive cyber-programs. Foreign nations have begun to include information warfare in their military doctrine, as well as their war college curricula, with respect to both defensive and offensive applications.[37]

When outer and cyber spaces are conceived first and foremost as global commons, the international law on the use of force can be seen as largely irrelevant. The relevant law is the law governing economic rights and non-intervention, not the law of self-defence. As US President Barack Obama noted in 2011, international law would play a role in US cyber security planning. However, in its *International Strategy for Cyberspace* the same year US Government elaborated a much broader stance noting that: '[w]hen warranted, the United States will respond to hostile acts in cyber space as we would to any other threat to our country.'[38] The strategy document went on to note that all States possess an inherent right to self-defence overtly intimating that outer and cyber space activities did not mean that the response was confined to the same pathways of action but the full set of military actions available with its ominous reservation that the US reserves 'the right to use all *necessary means* – diplomatic, informational, military, and economic – as appropriate and consistent with applicable international law, in order to defend our Nation, our allies, our partners, and our interests'.[39]

16 *Use of force*

In this context, contestation is raised by the 'all necessary means' phrase since States are pursuing government-sponsored offensive cyber-programs often under the broad context of self-preservation and national interest. This is buttressed by the fact that major and medium military powers have progressively included (and now enshrine) Information Warfare (IW) in their military doctrine. This points to the fact that they recognise the value of attacking adversary computer systems in order to counter other States' military superiority. Several major military powers (including Russia, China and France) have acknowledged developing IW programs. This is not confined to the major powers but also to medium and other ascendant powers. By one estimate, three dozen States are or have established sophisticated electronic intrusion programs.[40] As Serabian notes:

> nations developing cyber-programs recognise the value of attacking adversary computer systems, both on the military and domestic front. Just as foreign governments and the military services have long emphasised the need to disrupt the flow of information in combat situations, they now stress the power of cyber-warfare when targeted against civilian infrastructures, particularly those that could support military strategy.[41]

Sophisticated electronic intrusion is now a threat to national security and emergency preparedness in broad spectra that include telecommunications and information systems.[42] Military powers are building capacity and developing strategies in the arena of outer and cyber information frameworks. Thus, these digital commons are viewed through the prism of conventional and non-conventional war fighting in mind. Many recognise that attacks on information infrastructure and processes can have catastrophic consequences.

Commencing in 2006, the North Atlantic Treaty Organisation (NATO) began running operational cyber defence capabilities and establishing deployment models on the operating of cyber defence technologies and capabilities.[43] This culminated in the 2010 *NATO Strategic Concept* in which the Alliance commits to

> develop further [its] ability to prevent, detect, defend against and recover from cyber attacks, including by using the NATO planning process to enhance and coordinate national cyber-defence capabilities, bringing all NATO bodies under centralized cyber protection, and better integrating NATO cyber awareness, warning and response with member nations.[44]

In 2011, the wide mandate given to the US Cyber Command (which among other mandates includes defending DoD information networks) echoed that it should be prepared to conduct full-spectrum military cyber space operations in all domains to ensure US/Allied freedom of action in cyber space while curtailing the ability of adversaries.[45]

Conclusion

This chapter has broadly sketched the legal challenges that regulating the global digital commons pose under the extant regime on the use of force and its original basis and focus on kinetic (physical) force. Chapters 2 and 3 will flesh out the common and uncommon legal and operational issues. The basis is that cross-border clandestine acts can often be at the periphery of the mainstream legal framework. Activities in the digital commons occur in interconnected and complex environments. Often, the same pathways used to conduct peaceful and routine operations serve as the conduits for force multiplication through integration of weaponry platforms in highly coordinated events. On the other hand existing law that might seem applicable to cyber warfare can be inadequate because of the unique characteristics of cyber space as a tool for warcraft as it does not fit neatly into the current international law structure. The laws regulating the initiation of armed conflict are often inadequate in conflicts where the injury is non-kinetic, meaning that attributing actions to a State poses a difficult challenge.[46]

In sum, the law surrounding outer space and cyber space warfare initiatives has not developed as quickly as the threat it now poses. Among the many challenges is the confusion in how laws or frameworks should regulate hostile intrusions in the digital commons since the Law of Armed Conflict was specifically designed to prevent kinetic attacks, not the destruction of information. Second, attributing a hostile intrusion to a State usually extremely difficult. This means that even though the law on State responsibility is generally clear, the failure to definitively allocate blame curtails what proportionate penalties may be feasible. This is considering that some forms of outer and cyber space intrusions or interference can be seen as lawful within the context of international law. The more practical question is how best to develop concrete rules of engagement for actual application using both existing and analogical frameworks. Several questions arise: Does the existing process for developing rules for the use of military forces adequately accommodate computer network attack? What can guide militaries in developing rules for potential weaponisation of outer space?

In the next chapter, a detailed articulation of the basic parameters of the information RMA flagging the significant legal and policy gap between 'technical capabilities emerging from the laboratories – and the policy and legal architecture to support them'[47] will be undertaken. The highlights of Chapter 2 will be subsequently discussed sequentially in Chapters 3 and 4, which respectively deal with outer space and cyber space.

Notes

1 Chatham House (2005) 'Principles of International Law on the Use of Force by States in Self-Defence', Working Paper, ILP WP 05/0, 6, available at www.chathamhouse.org/publications/papers/view/108106 (accessed 23 April 2013).

2 *UN Charter*, 26 June 1945, 59 Stat. 1031, 892 UNTS 119, Article 2(4).
3 Ibid., emphasis added.
4 In other words, 'integrity' has to be read as 'inviolability', proscribing any kind of forcible trespassing.
5 For instance, at the San Francisco Conference, a proposal by Brazil of 6 May 1945 to extend the prohibition of force to economic coercion was explicitly rejected.
6 *Declaration Concerning Friendly Relations*, GA Res 2625, UN GAOR, 25th sess, 1883rd plen mtg, UN Doc A/RES/2625 (1970).
7 Apart from that, the Declaration stipulates as a further principle the obligation not to intervene in matters within the domestic jurisdiction of another State. It is in this context that the Declaration (ibid) reads: 'No State may use or encourage the use of economic, political or any other type of measures to coerce another State.' By doing so, the Declaration underlines the fact that the scope of Article 2(4) is restricted to armed force. Economic and other types of coercion are not covered by Article 2(4) but by the general principle of non-intervention.
8 Simpson, G. (2014) 'Principles of International Law on the Use of Force by States in Self-Defence', Working Paper, ILP WP 05/0, 18, [online] available at www.chathamhouse.org/publications/papers/view/108106 (accessed 23 April 2014, emphasis added).
9 Waxman, M.C. (2011) 'Cyber Attacks and the Use of Force: Back to the Future of Article 2(4)', *Yale Journal of International Law*, 36(2): 421, 428.
10 See e.g. *Military and Paramilitary Activities In and Against Nicaragua* (*Nicaragua v. US*), 1986 ICJ Rep 14, 214–16 (June 27); Dinstein, Y. (1994, 2nd edn) *War, Aggression, and Self-Defence*. Cambridge: Cambridge University Press, 193–6 (using the 'scale and effects' test from the *Nicaragua* case to assess armed attacks).
11 *Definition of Aggression*, G.A. Res. 3314, Annex, art. 2, UN GAOR, 29th Sess., UN Doc. A/RES/3314/Annex (14 December 1974) (noting that the uses of force 'shall constitute *prima facie* evidence of an act of aggression although the Security Council may . . . conclude that a determination that an act of aggression has been committed would not be justified in the light of other relevant circumstances, including the fact that the acts concerned or their consequences are not of sufficient gravity').
12 Ibid.
13 Thus what constitutes an armed attack encompasses the following acts, either individually or in combination:

   a) *Invasion, bombardment and cross-border shooting*. These examples represent the classic cases of armed attacks, provided 'that the military actions are on a certain scale and have a major effect, and are thus not to be considered mere frontier incidents.'
   b) *Blockade*. An effective blocking of a State's ports or coasts by the armed forces of another State is an armed attack. The barring of passage for land-locked States to the open sea across another State's territory has not been accepted as an armed attack.
   c) *Attack on the land, sea or air forces or on the civilian marine and air fleets*. An armed attack occurs when the armed forces of one State attack the land, sea, or air forces, or the civilian marine and air fleets, of another State. The regular forces of a State, wherever they are, always have the right to defend themselves by military force.
   d) *Breach of stationing agreements*. An armed attack may occur when a State uses its armed forces within the territory of another State in contravention of the conditions provided for in the agreement, or any

extension of their presence beyond the termination of the agreement; provided, however, that the breach of the terms of the agreement has the effect of an invasion or occupation.

e) *Placing territory at another State's disposal*. The voluntary action of a state in allowing another State to use its territory for committing an armed attack is also an armed attack.

f) *Participation in the use of force by military organized unofficial groups*. It is widely accepted that indirect force falls under the definition of armed attack. The sending of armed bands to use force in another State makes the armed bands a *de facto* State agent, thus the sending State has engaged in an armed attack. Similarly, 'substantial involvement' in the activities of an armed band may also constitute an armed attack.

(Simma, B. (ed.) (1994) *The Charter of the United Nations: A Commentary*. Oxford: Oxford University Press, 111–26)

14 Ian Brownlie (1963) has categorised several Article exceptions to the restrictions on the use of force. They are as follows:

i) acts of self–defence;
ii) acts of collective self–defence;
iii) actions authorised by a competent national organ (e.g. the United Nations Security Council);
iv) actions where treaties confer rights to intervene by an ad hoc invitation, or where consent is given by the territorial sovereign;
v) actions to terminate trespass;
vi) necessity arising from natural catastrophe; and
vii) measures to protect the lives or property of a State's nationals in a foreign territory.

15 Brownlie, I. (1963) *International Law and the Use of Force by States*. Oxford: Clarendon Press, 432–3.

16 *UN Charter*, 26 June 1945, 59 Stat. 1031, 892 UNTS 119, Article 51.

17 Russell, R. (1958) *A History of the UN Charter: The Role of the United States, 1940–1945*. Washington, DC: Brookings Institution, 698–9.

18 See Condron, S. (1999) 'Justification for Unilateral Action in Response to the Iraqi Threat: A Critical Analysis of Operation Desert Fox', *Military Law Review*, 161: 115, 151–5; see also Dinstein, Y. (1994, 2nd edn) *War, Aggression, and Self-Defence*. Cambridge: Cambridge University Press, 202 (drawing the distinction between imminence and immediacy).

19 See e.g. Stone, J. (1958) *Aggression and World Order: A Critique of United Nations Theories of Aggression*. Sydney: Maitland, 94–5.

20 See e.g. Brownlie, I. (1963) *International Law and the Use of Force by States*. Oxford: Clarendon Press, 279.

21 Waxman, M.C. (2011) 'Cyberattacks and the Use of Force: Back to the Future of Article 2(4)', *Yale Journal of International Law*, 36(2): 421, 428.

22 Ibid., 421, 430.

23 Blum, Y. (1986) 'The Legality of State Response to Acts of Terrorism', in Benjamin Netanyahu (ed.) *Terrorism: How the West Can Win*. New York: Farrar, Straus & Giroux, 137.

24 See Moore, J. (1906) *A Digest of International Law as Embodied in Diplomatic Discussions, Treaties and other International Agreements, International Awards, the Decisions of Municipal Courts, and the Writings of Jurists* (Vol. 2). Washington, DC: US Government Print Office, 409–14.

25 Ibid.

26 Stone, J. (1958) *Aggression and World Order: A Critique of United Nations Theories of Aggression*. Sydney: Maitland, 245.
27 Crimes of War Project, Byers, M. (2003) 'Iraq and the "Bush Doctrine" of Pre-emptive Self-Defence', [online] available at www.crimesofwar.org/expert/bush-byers.html (accessed 10 December 2003).
28 Crimes of War Project, Koskiennemi, M. (2003) 'Iraq and the "Bush Doctrine" of Pre-emptive Self-Defence' ([online] available at www.crimesofwar.org/expert/bush-koskenniemi.html (accessed 10 December 2003).
29 Ibid.
30 Shaw, M. (2014) 'Principles of International Law on the Use of Force by States in Self-Defence', Working Paper, ILP WP 05/0, 17–18, [online] available at www.chathamhouse.org/publications/papers/view/108106 (accessed 23 April 2014, emphasis added).
31 Waxman, M.C. (2011) 'Cyber Attacks and the Use of Force: Back to the Future of Article 2(4)', *Yale Journal of International Law*, 36(2): 421, 428–9.
32 See e.g. Schachter, O. (1984) 'International Law: The Right of States to Use Armed Force', *Michigan Law Review*, 82: 1620, 1624.
33 *UN Charter*, 26 June 1945, 59 Stat. 1031, 892 UNTS 119, Article 2(4).
34 News24.com (2003) 'China looking at "space force"' [online] available at www.news24.com/News24/Technology/News/0,,2-13-1443_1433115,00.html (accessed 10 May 2006).
35 Ibid.
36 See e.g. Joyner, C.C. and Lotrionte, C. (2001) 'Information Warfare as International Coercion: Elements of a Legal Framework', *European Journal of International Law*, 12(5): 825, 828.
37 Statement for the Record by Serabian, J.A. (2000) 'Information Operations Issue Manager, Central Intelligence Agency before the Joint Economic Committee on Cyber Threats and the US Economy', [online] available at www.odci.gov/cia/publicaffairs/speeches/cyberthreats022300.html (accessed 18 February 2013).
38 Executive Office of the President (2011) 'International Strategy for Cyberspace: Prosperity, Security, and Openness in a Networked World', [online] available at www.whitehouse.gov/sites/default/files/rss_viewer/international_strategy_for_cyber space.pdf (accessed 20 June 2012) (emphasis added).
39 Ibid.
40 See e.g. Joyner, C.C. and Lotrionte, C. (2001) 'Information Warfare as International Coercion: Elements of a Legal Framework', *European Journal of International Law*, 12(5): 825, 831–2.
41 Statement for the Record by Serabian, J.A. (2000) 'Information Operations Issue Manager, Central Intelligence Agency before the Joint Economic Committee on Cyber Threats and the US Economy', [online] available at www.odci.gov/cia/publicaffairs/speeches/cyberthreats022300.html (accessed 18 February 2013).
42 Madsen, W. (1993) 'Intelligence Agency Threats to Computer Security', *International Journal of Intelligence and Counter Intelligence*, 6: 446–87.
43 NATO (2011) 'Working with the Private Sector to Deter Cyber Attacks', [online] available at www.nato.int/cps/en/natolive/news_80764.htm (accessed 20 June 2012).
44 NATO (2010) 'Strategic Concept for the Defence and Security of the Members of the North Atlantic Treaty Organization', 19, [online] available at www.nato.int/lisbon2010/strategic-concept-2010-eng.pdf (accessed 20 June 2012).
45 Lynn, W. (2011) 'Announcement of the Department of Defense Cyberspace Strategy at the National Defense University', [online] available at www.pentagon channel.mil/onestory_popup.aspx?pid=FttPuXny5i7D8p1hC0rgnXrveieDVeMW (accessed 20 June 2012).

46 See e.g. Hunker, J., Hutchinson, B. and Margulies, J. (2008) 'Role and Challenges for Sufficient Cyber-Attack Attribution' *Institute for Information Infrastructure Protection, White Paper*, [online] available at www.thei3p.org.library.newcastle.edu.au/docs/publications/whitepaper-attribution.pdf (accessed 12 September 2012).
47 O'Donnell, B.T. and Kraska, J.C. (2002) 'Humanitarian Law: Developing International Rules for the Digital Battlefield', *Journal of Conflict & Security Law*, 8(1): 133, 140.

2 Revolution in military affairs
Hi-tech weaponry, low-tech legal safeguards

Introduction

In the twenty-first century, the reliance on digital ecosystems stands to give the side with information dominance a major and potentially decisive advantage in not just offensive and defensive military operations but also similar operations in protecting civilian and military CNI. The ever increasing efficient application of military force is increasingly influenced by the ability to collect, transmit and interpret information. This underpins the practicality of States conducting military operations without constraints of distance, terrain or weather.

Military and civilian operations are increasingly reliant upon automated and semi-automated systems both in peacetime and wartime given the rapid accumulation of technology at their disposal. Information operations include a myriad of actions. Activities include, but are not limited to, those taken to achieve information superiority by affecting adversary information, information-based processes, information systems and computer-based networks.[1] As a baseline, the following activities have also been identified as falling within the broad framework of information operations: military deception, electronic warfare, computer network attack and defence.[2]

The next two sections of this chapter will examine the parameters of outer and cyber spaces in the development of new forms of military activities and operations. The focus will be on emerging and ascendant technologies and how this impacts on the general mantra that these arenas should be confined to peaceful, non-military purposes. The aim is to set the stage for the subsequent nuanced analysis.

The fourth domain: outer space

Leaps in space technologies commencing in the twentieth century have put the development of space weapons within the realm of possibility for several States. In 1995 as the twentieth century drew to a close the US released its *New World Vistas: Air and Space Power for the 21st Century Report*. In the report, the United States Air Force (USAF) noted:

In the next two decades, new technologies will allow the fielding of space-based weapons of devastating effectiveness to be used to deliver energy and mass as force projection in tactical and strategic conflict. These advances will enable lasers with reasonable mass and cost to affect very many kills.[3]

In 1998, the United States Space Command (USSPACECOM) released its *Long Range Plan: Implementing USSPACECOM Vision for 2020*. This outlined the US military's vision regarding control of space and developing a capacity to project force from space. The first two mission statements of USSPACECOM's *Vision For 2020* noted the significance of 'space support' and 'force enhancement', essentially the use of space assets to facilitate military operations of combat forces on land, sea and air.[4] The next two mission statements – 'space control' and 'force application' – are more controversial as they suggest the weaponisation of space, and are most closely related to combat in a future theatre of military space operations. Overall, the four mission areas encapsulate 'space control'.[5] The following year the US DoD expanded upon and reinforced themes raised by USSPACECOM's *Vision for 2020*, stating that:

[p]urposeful interference with US space systems will be viewed as an infringement on our sovereign rights. The US may take all appropriate self-defense measures, including, if directed by the National Command Authorities, the use of force, to respond to such an infringement on US rights.[6]

The relentless drive to develop outer space weapons by the US has also spurred other military powers to craft ambitious space programs in part driven by military considerations. A measure of how far space militarisation and potential weaponisation has progressed is readily apparent by the establishment in 2001 by the USAF of a space directorate to oversee the operations of two activated space squadrons: the 76th Space Control Squadron and the 527th Space Aggressor Squadron.[7] This has established a space force organised as a component of the US military (Army, Navy and Air Force) under the overall control of USSPACECOM.[8] Building on this focus, in September 2002 the US Administration issued a landmark national security policy paper, which emphasised the need for '[i]nnovation within the armed forces [which] will rest on experimentation with new approaches to warfare, strengthening joint operations, exploiting US intelligence advantages, and taking full advantage of science and technology'.[9] As an integral part of the policy, US DoD is focused on maintaining technological supremacy so as to 'dominate the space dimension of military operations'.[10] The policy went on to note that this encompasses 'the ability to defend the homeland, conduct information operations, ensure US access to distant theaters, and protect critical US infrastructure and assets in outer space'.[11]

The emerging arms race by military powers to gain and maintain space superiority in the twenty-first century is in part anchored by the convergence of air, land and sea power functions through integrated battleground platforms. The development of offensive counter-space capabilities seeks to provide military commanders with new combat tools. The net result is spurring aggressive research and development of innovative space weapons with the capability of delivering and deploying ordnances from space through low-Earth orbit (LEO), geo-synchronous orbit (GEO) and sun-synchronous orbit (SSO). While one of the strongest immediate motivations for ambitious space programs may be seen as national prestige, the basic reality is the contribution to developing, harnessing and generating extra capacity for military systems.[12] Essentially then, outer space as a war theatre is the focus of serious planning as the militaries of major powers brace for new forms of high-tech combat in the twenty-first century.

Developments by military powers are indicative of a rapidly expanding perception among them of the centrality of information systems in support of military operations in ever increasing complex digital frameworks. This perception is being translated into reality by the very significant resources now devoted by each of them to the development in defensive and offensive activities underpinned by information frameworks and aspects of outer space capabilities, such as Global Positioning Systems (GPS), remote sensing and multi-dimensional reconnaissance and surveillance. Without wishing to appear melodramatic, the prospect of a celestial war can no longer be regarded as mere fantasy. Just as States have already been undertaking what might be termed passive military activities in outer space since the advent of space technology, outer space is now increasingly seen as part of active engagement in the conduct of armed conflict.[13] A harbinger of things to come was flagged in 2001 by a Commission chaired by Donald Rumsfeld – then US Secretary of Defence. After a comprehensive space review, it reported back to the US Congress.[14] The Report warned that the 600 satellites on which the US States military depends upon for photo reconnaissance, targeting, communications, weather forecasting, early warning and intelligence gathering were highly vulnerable to attack from adversaries.[15] To reduce the nation's vulnerability, the Rumsfeld Commission urged the government to develop 'superior space capabilities', including the ability to 'negate the hostile use of space against United States interests' by using 'power projection in, from and through space.'[16] It noted that from history every medium – air, land and sea – had seen conflict. The report rounded off by calling space warfare a virtual certainty.[17]

The fifth domain: cyber space

There is a broad range of capabilities to attack computer networks that are in various stages of development and testing. Other capabilities are already being employed in actual operations by a growing number of States. In 2001, a computer worm named 'Code Red' swept across the globe in two different waves.[18] The first wave infected tens of thousands of computers. So severe was the attack that the US Pentagon temporarily blocked public access to its website and forced the White House to change its numerical Internet address as a precautionary measure.[19] A second wave spread a new variant of the worm a week later and infected over 150,000 computers.[20] The worm defaced websites with the words 'Hacked by Chinese'.[21] No one took credit for the 'Code Red' attack.[22] China strenuously denied any governmental involvement. Responses by affected States were just as unclear because of the ambiguity of the applicable international laws that apply to computer attacks raising as it does whether the scope, duration and intensity would be sufficient to qualify this intrusion as an armed attack, since armed attacks and imminent armed attacks remain the recognised triggers that allow States to respond in self-defence. It is of note that China's military possesses a dedicated military department – the Third Department – whose mandate includes cyber surveillance, and Computer Network Exploitation (CNE).[23] The Department's Seventh Bureau (61580 Unit) is responsible for CNE specialising in computer network defense and attack and mapping of Third States' digital networks and processes.[24] A US Pentagon Report in 2007 on China's military force indicates that it is developing tactics to achieve electromagnetic dominance early in a conflict.[25] The Report added that China, while not yet having a formal doctrine of electronic warfare at that stage was progressively considering offensive cyber attacks within its operational exercises with a robust move to incorporate cyber warfare in organisation, training and doctrine.[26]

In 2007, an even more multifaceted real-life impact of cyber attacks over a State's digital ecosystem was manifested when hackers (strongly believed to be Russian) unleashed a cyber-assault on Estonia, temporarily shutting down Estonian government computers, after the Baltic country caused offense by re-burying a Russian soldier from World War II. The following year, in advance of the brief Russo-Georgian, cyber attacks preceded the eventual kinetic invasion of Georgia. The cyber attacks began weeks before a single mortar was dropped in the conflict with Russia.[27] This time, the cyber attacks disabled numerous government websites and information pathways of Georgia.[28] In particular, the operations focused on governmental ministry servers, which were overrun and crippled with attacks necessitating the government to re-route communication with the world through blogs and websites of Third States.[29] The timing was very suspicious.[30] These acts of 'cyber warfare' committed against Georgia and Estonia gave the world a glimpse of the future of conflict in the fifth domain and the impact of constraining an adversary's capability to effectively operate and respond, but significantly the disruption of regional and international peace and security.

It is largely not in question that military powers are developing offensive information operations as a tool for their military commanders as evidenced by changing military doctrines, rules of engagement and tactics. There is no novelty in the fact that manipulation of information has always been employed during armed conflict as a part of military Operations Other than War (OOTW) in support of overt and covert national security activities. However, the quandary is the use in grey areas between non-hostile and hostile operations. This is considering that the potential of IW has been fostered by the proliferation of information systems, in particular the convergence of computers and telecommunications, which has deepened and broadened information infrastructures. Thus, information operations are increasing curving a niche as an independent war-fighting tool. In this regard, Toby Friesen notes that:

> Cyberspace has emerged as a warfighting domain not unlike land, sea, and air, and we are engaged in a less visible, but none-the-less critical battle against sophisticated cyber space attacks . . . Our adversaries seek to operate from behind technical, legal, and international screens as they execute their costly attacks.[31]

Consider that the US DoD speaks of 'actions taken to achieve information superiority by affecting adversary information, information-based processes, information systems, and computer-based networks while leveraging and defending one's own information'.[32] Equally its main and traditional ally, the United Kingdom's (UK) Ministry of Defence (MoD) speaks of the need to not only constrain but also defang 'deliberate . . . and systematic attacks on critical information activities' which seek to exploit, modify, corrupt information or to deny service. These standpoints share a commonality, namely the ability to neutralise intrusive activities that degrade information systems, processes and physical telecommunications plus the capability to strike back vigorously.

With the concern over computer network defence, policy planners, particularly in the military, are also equally enthusiastic on the potential advantages to be gained in military operations by offensive attacks against an adversary's information infrastructure.[33] The pivot is that information infrastructure is made up of myriad communications networks that interlink at many different levels. This means that the convergence of civilian and military network nodes means multiple gains with small-scale but robust intrusions. As Brian O'Donnell and James Kraska note '[f]or the strategic planner or senior military planner, network attack is inviting generally because it is less harmful to non-combatants and civilian infrastructure, reducing civilian casualties that are too often a bitter consequence of international politics'.[34]

Conclusion

The utility and centrality of satellites is poignantly stated in the 2006 *US Quadrennial Defense Review*. The author quotes this at some length below

28 *Revolution in military affairs*

as it interconnects the utility of outer and cyber spaces. In the review, it was noted that:

> The foundation for net-centric operations is the Global Information Grid [GIG], a globally interconnected, end-to-end set of trusted and protected information networks. The GIG optimizes the processes for collecting, processing, storing, disseminating, managing and sharing information within the Department and with other partners ... It has deployed an enhanced land-based network and new satellite constellation as part of the Transformational Communication Architecture [TCA] to provide high-bandwidth, survivable internet protocol communications. Together, they will support battle-space awareness, time-sensitive targeting and communications on the move.[35]

The essence is that attacks via outer and cyber space are designed to disrupt, deny, degrade, or destroy information. The unique nature of the threat and the ability for militarisation and weaponisation of outer and cyber spaces to inflict physical and non-physical injury through space and time strains traditional definitions of the use of force. The utility of the digital commons will increase rapidly rather than recede since through them modern militaries can conduct high-tempo effective operations assured by communication networks undergirded by outer and cyber space assets. It is in this regard that States continue to spend billions of dollars on research and development as they robustly reconfigure their militaries and rewrite their military doctrines and training manuals. It is to be expected that the more new technological breakthroughs magnify the benefits of military operations not faced with the strictures of distance, terrain and weather the more States will get increasingly more intransigent on regulation, which would mean giving up a magical platform.

Notes

1 See Joint Chiefs of Staff (2001) *Department of Defence Dictionary of Military and Associated Terms (Joint Publication 1–02)*. Washington, DC: US Department of Defence, 253.
2 See e.g. Joint Chiefs of Staff (1998) *Department of Defence Joint Doctrine for Information Operations (I–9 Joint Publication 3–13)*. Washington, DC: US Department of Defence.
3 United States. USAF Scientific Advisory Board (1995) *New World Vistas: Air and Space Power for the 21st Century Report*. Washington, DC: US Department of Defence.
4 US Space Command (1998) *Long Range Plan: Implementing USSPACECOM Vision for 2020*. Peterson Air Force Base, Colorado Springs, CO.
5 Ibid.
6 US Department of Defence (1999) 'Directive Number 3100.10' § 4.2.1', [online] available at www.dtic.mil/whs/directives/corres/pdf/310010p.pdf (accessed 24 December 2012).

7 Ricks, T. (2001) 'Space is Playing Field for Newest War Game: Air Force Exercise Shows Shift in Focus', *Washington Post*, 29 January, 1.
8 See generally US Space Command (2001) 'US Air Force Space Command: Command News', [online] available at www.spacecom.af.mil/hqafspc/news/default.htm (accessed 16 April 2011).
9 The White House (2002) *The National Security of the United States of America*, [online] available at www.whitehouse.gov/nsc/nss.html (accessed 20 July 2011).
10 See Mosteshar, S. (2004) 'Militarization of Outer Space: Legality and Implications for the Future of Space Law', *Proceedings of the Colloquium on the Law of Outer Space*, 47: 473–80, footnotes 1 and 2.
11 The White House (2002) *The National Security of the United States of America*, [online] available at www.whitehouse.gov/nsc/nss.html (accessed 20 July 2011).
12 David, L. (2003) 'Pentagon Report: China's Space Warfare Tactics Aimed at US Supremacy', *Space*, 1 August, [online] available at www.space.com/news/china_dod_030801.html (accessed 23 January 2012).
13 See Ricks, T. (2001) 'Space is Playing Field for Newest War Game; Air Force Exercise Shows Shift in Focus', *Washington Post*, 29 January, A1.
14 *Report of the Commission to Assess United States National Security Space Management and Organization* (2001), [online] available at www.defenselink.mil/pubs/space20010111.html (accessed 24 December 2012).
15 Ibid.
16 Ibid.
17 Ibid.
18 See Wong, N.C. (2001) '"Code Red" Creeping Worldwide', *Washington Post*, 2 August, E1.
19 See Editorial (2001) 'Pentagon Web Sites Blocked; Threat of "Code Red" Computer "Worm" Prompts Safeguards', *Washington Post*, 24 July, A5.
20 See Wong, N.C. (2001) '"Code Red" Creeping Worldwide', *Washington Post*, 2 August, E1 (describing the second incarnation of the Code Red worm).
21 See Editorial (2001) 'Pentagon Web Sites Blocked; Threat of "Code Red" Computer "Worm" Prompts Safeguards', *Washington Post*, 24 July, A5 (describing the damage caused by the worm).
22 See Wong, N.C. (2001) '"Code Red" Creeping Worldwide', *Washington Post*, 2 August, E1 (reporting a lack of indication regarding the worm's origin).
23 Minnick, W. (2011) 'China's PLA Involved in Cyber Espionage: Report', [online] available at www.defensenews.com/article/20111110/DEFSECT04/111100310/China-s-PLA-Involved-Cyber-Espionage-Report (accessed 4 May 2014).
24 Ibid.
25 See Fidler, S. et al. (2007) 'US Concedes Danger of Cyber-attack', *Financial Times Online*. 7 September, [online] available at http://0-search.ft.com.library.newcastle.edu.au/ftArticle?queryText=People%27s+Liberation+Army%2C+computer&aje=false& id=070905010503&ct=0 (accessed 17 May 2012).
26 See Friesen, T.L. (2009) 'Resolving Tomorrow's Conflicts Today: How New Developments within the UN Security Council can be Used to Combat Cyberwarfare', *Naval Law Review*, 58: 89, 97; Creekman, D.M. (2002) 'A Helpless America? An Examination of the Legal Options Available to the United States in Response to Various Cyber-attacks from China', *American University International Law Review*, 17(3): 641, 670–1.
27 Anonymous (2008) 'War, Redefined; Even Before Russian Troops Arrived, Georgian Government Websites Were Under Cyber Attack', *Los Angeles Times*, 17 August, Part A, p. 25.
28 See Markoff, J. (2008b) 'Georgia Takes a Beating in the Cyberwar with Russia', *New York Times Online*, 11 August, [online] available at http://bits.blogs.

30 *Revolution in military affairs*

nytimes.com/2008/08/11/georgia-takes-a-beating-in-the-cyberwar-with-russia/?scp=1&sq=cyberwarfare&st=cse (accessed 5 November 2012).
29 See Markoff, J. (2008a) 'Before the Gunfire, Cyberattacks', *New York Times*, 13 August, A1, [online] available at http://www.nytimes.com/2008/08/13/technology/13cyber.html (accessed 1 August 2011).
30 Ibid.
31 See Toby L. Friesen (2009) 'Resolving Tomorrow's Conflicts Today: How New Developments within the UN Security Council can be Used to Combat Cyberwarfare', *Naval Law Review*, 58: 89–90.
32 US Air Force Cyber Command (n.d.) *Cyberspace 101, Understanding the Cyberspace Domain*, [online] available at www.afcyber.af.mil/library/factsheets/factsheet.asp?id=10784 (accessed 1 August 2013, on file with author).
33 See e.g. Brian T. O'Donnell and James C. Kraska (2002) 'Humanitarian Law: Developing International Rules for the Digital Battlefield', *Journal of Conflict and Security Law*, 8(1): 133, 138.
34 Ibid.
35 US Department of Defence (2006) *US Quadrennial Defense Review Report*, Washington, DC: Department of Defence, 58, [online] available at www.defense.gov/home/features/2014/0314_sdr/qdr.aspx (accessed 15 January 2014).

3 The fourth domain

Ascendance of outer space as a war theatre

Introduction

The use of satellites in communication, navigation, space flight, meteorology, remote sensing, disaster reduction and other fields of science and technology is now indispensable. While achieving notable progress in the peaceful uses of outer space, humanity is faced nevertheless with its ever-expanding use for military purposes. Because of its uniquely commanding height, outer space has gained military and strategic value as a platform for warfare. More than half of all spacecraft presently orbiting the Earth serve military purposes and this will only increase as ascendant space powers develop satellite constellation to rival or equalise that of established space powers. The irony is that leading space faring powers (inevitably also the major military powers) have and still describe all their space missions as 'peaceful'.[1] The crux of the matter though is that all too often space craft and devices have dual capabilities – civilian and military, defensive and offensive.[2]

In this chapter, the basic tenets of the *UN Charter* on the regime on the use force will be interwoven with the extant and relevant legal provisions of the Space Law regime. The regime is comprised of a cluster of treaties, which will be highlighted as the chapter unfolds. The author wishes to state at the outset that this chapter's remit is not a detailed analysis of *all* outer space treaties. This is not in any way to side-line other instruments and declarations, but rather is a framework that avoids raising the entire body of Space Law when clearly some of the instruments are highly particularistic and not germane to the book's central themes. The focus is on significant provisions drawn from the various instruments that have relevance to outer space's militarisation and weaponisation.[3]

'Peaceful': easy understanding or difficult enunciation

The US (a pioneering space power) has, from the very beginning of the Space Age up to the present, maintained the official position that 'peaceful' means 'non-aggressive' and not 'non-military'.[4] Some of the very earliest statements by the US on the international control of space activities appear to support the proposition that outer space should be used exclusively for non-military purposes.[5] A main goal of US space policy during the pre-*Outer Space Treaty*[6] era was to gain international recognition of the legality of reconnaissance satellites, while simultaneously discouraging military space activities that threatened those assets.[7] Ivan Vlasic notes that '[t]he term "peaceful purposes" ... was interpreted by the United States to mean ... [that] all military uses are permitted and lawful as long as they remain "non-aggressive" as per Article 2(4) of the *UN Charter*, which prohibits "the threat or use of force"'.[8]

The then Union of Soviet Socialist Republics – USSR – (Soviet Union – another pioneering space power) also took the view in the 1950s that 'peaceful purposes' meant 'non-military', and that all military activities in space were thus prohibited. The Soviets, much like the Americans, initially maintained that all of their activities in space were 'peaceful' and 'scientific'. However, by the spring of 1958 (less than a year after the launch of Sputnik I – the first ever artificial satellite placed in outer space by the Soviet Union) the anticipation of the reconnaissance and surveillance military capabilities of satellites triggered a decisive shift in the Soviets' policy towards the view that space could and should be used for 'peaceful purposes'. The Soviet Union's official line hardened as its military satellite programme matured.

In the background of the US and Soviet Union contestation regarding the meaning of 'peaceful', the international community was moving to establish a regulatory framework of specific guidelines premised on the fundamental principle of 'peaceful' purposes. This at first glance seems to militate against any sort of militarisation or weaponisation operations.[9] However, as will be discussed in this chapter, key provisions of international treaties and declarations readily lend themselves to interpretations that would support many aspects of militarisation and weaponisation of outer space. The matter, when coupled with the lacunae present in the relevant Space Law treaties, means that the regime can be malleable depending on the perspective a State adopts owing to the flexibility in interpretation.[10] After all it is a fundamental axiom of international law (and law generally) that if an act is not specifically prohibited, it is permitted.

The intersection of the *UN Charter* regime on force and Outer Space Law

Whether a particular technology is permitted in outer space depends upon the intended use of the technology and whether it is to be used in the vacuum of outer space or on the surface of a celestial body such as the moon. The military origin or potential military use of a particular technology is not a factor[11] with the exception of weapons of mass destruction, which are considered aggressive and therefore explicitly prohibited in space and on celestial bodies.[12] However, non-aggressive military uses of outer space (as opposed to celestial bodies) are not prohibited meaning military equipment and personnel may be used for peaceful purposes even on the moon and other celestial bodies.[13]

Closing the loop? Network centric warfare matures

In 1990, the first Gulf War ('Operation Desert Storm') heralded the beginning of a new era in the dynamics of waging war.[14] Coalition forces, which included the largest naval fleet constituted since World War II, were supported by 'the most sophisticated information network ever designed ... dwarfing anything generated in previous wars'.[15] An impressive array of technologies, and particularly the use of satellites and other outer-space mounted devices, was on display. The US (and its allies) demonstrated that information technology would operationally be harnessed to coordinate land, sea and aerial military assets to produce a holistic integrated battle platform. The 'Smart War' featured lightening attacks targeting Iraqi command and control targets,[16] and 'microwave' technology targeting and jamming Iraqi command and control facilities.[17] The effectiveness of the integrated battleground platform underpinned by information technology and smart weaponry epitomised the importance of high-tech warfare and the ability of sophisticated space-based command, control, communications and intelligence systems to link land, sea and air assets and forces.[18]

In light of the various spectrums of space militarisation and weaponisation, two cleavages are evident – direct military force (here meaning physical space devices which make actual proximate contact with their targets) and indirect force (here meaning the use of space weaponry that makes contact with space assets through space by the use of shock waves, electromagnetic pulses, radiation belts and/or laser beams). This positional observation forms the basis of the next sections of the chapter through a juxtaposition of the tenets of the regime on the use of force and relevant provisions of the various outer space law instruments. As noted in the Introduction to this chapter, the specific focus is on provisions that directly or tangentially relate to the themes of this book.

Direct military force in outer space

Kinetic energy weapons are hypervelocity weapons and the most common form of direct force space weaponry, which have been under development and testing for years. They are within the capability of deployment by major military powers. Kinetic energy weapons of this nature derive their value as a weapon from their explosive capacity.[19] The most common species of kinetic energy weapons are ASATs. These act either through direct physical impact and explosion with space assets or by exploding in proximity to targets and generating lethal debris for impact. There are two general sub-types of this hypervelocity weaponry. One sub-type works by proximate explosion and is rocket launched to coincide with the same orbital plane as the target satellite. 'When in range an explosive charge aboard the interceptor is detonated, sending a cloud of shrapnel at high speed to destroy the target.'[20] The other sub-type of hypervelocity weaponry entails direct physical impact, normally the launching of a weapon directly targeting a space asset. While the Space Law regime generally provides that States have a right to deploy satellites and proscribes any interference, generally use of ASATs or Direct Energy Weapons – primarily lasers – specifically directed against a State's satellites would arguably be commensurate with the use of armed force by a State against the sovereignty of another State or perhaps would be equated with the with the use of weapons by a State against the territory of another State.

Indirect military force in outer space

Electromagnetic and radiation weapons with the capacity to impair electronic circuitry by the creation and/or emission of Electromagnetic Pulse (EMP) or radiation are the predominant form of indirect military force weaponry. Once generated, EMP and radiation are lethal to unprotected circuitry within a very large area and may also reduce the functions of space assets since they affect both radio and radar waves, important to the functions of satellites.[21] However, electromagnetic and radiation weapons are not the sole class of indirect force weaponry. Direct Energy Weapons (DEW), which include laser and radio frequency weapons, have also been under active research and development for decades and are now in operational deployment. They also operate along the same dynamic as electromagnetic and radiation weaponry by interfering with the functions and capabilities of space assets mainly through the 'blinding' of satellite sensors.

The next sections of this chapter will grapple with the nature of direct and indirect outer space weaponry through a juxtaposition of the nature of this weaponry within the framework of relevant provisions of the Space Law regime and in particular how the convergences and divergences of the regime of force intersect as well as deviate.

The *Outer Space Treaty*

During the seminal Outer Space Conference in 1960 the gathering laid the ground for the main treaties that underpin the Space Law regime to date:

> The question of whether to permit military equipment and personnel in space and on celestial bodies sparked a lively debate. Several delegations, including that of the Soviet Union, initially opposed even the peaceful use of military assets on celestial bodies.[22]

The US was of the persistent view that 'the use of military personnel and equipment for scientific research or any other peaceful purpose should not be prohibited'.[23] The basis not so much explicit was the prescient projection that the emerging new technology and engineering breakthrough developments had potentially significant military utility. The US averred that its position was simply a liberal allowance of military assets in space for peaceful purposes.[24] This view was supported by the UK. Ultimately, the Anglo-American view prevailed. The final treaty (which remains the bedrock of the cluster of Space Law treaties) – the *Outer Space Treaty* – embodied the understanding that the actual end-use of a piece of equipment used in space is more important than its military origin or potential military capabilities.[25]

The major principles governing activities in space are encapsulated in Articles I, II and III of the *Outer Space Treaty*.[26] Article I states that activities in outer space, including the moon and other celestial bodies, shall be conducted for the benefit of all countries and that outer space shall be part of the heritage of all mankind.[27] It also provides for freedom of scientific investigation in outer space and for international cooperation in endeavours.[28] Article II provides that nations cannot appropriate outer space by claim of sovereignty.[29] Article III provides that States Parties to the *Treaty* will conduct their activities in space in accordance with international law, the *UN Charter*, and in the interest of international peace, security, cooperation and understanding.[30]

Article III of the *Outer Space Treaty* is of particular significance with regard to the use of force with its reference to Article 51 of the *UN Charter* and in particular its implicit preservation of the right of States to use space in self-defence. It provides:

> States Parties to the *Treaty* shall carry on activities in the exploration and use of outer space, including the moon and other celestial bodies, in accordance with *international law, including the Charter of the United Nations*, in the interest of maintaining international peace and security and promoting international co-operation and understanding.[31]

Two significant observations arise from this provision. First, Article III applies the restrictions of all international law to outer space activities ('in accordance with'). As products of 'international law', this surely includes both the *jus ad bellum*, made obvious by Article III's specific reference to the *UN Charter*, and the *jus in bello*. This observation provides the strongest evidence that as far as its principles will apply to future technologies, the law of war has been incorporated into military space operations by virtue of the *Outer Space Treaty*. A second observation relates to the requirement that a State's exploration and use of outer space be 'in the interest of maintaining international peace and security'.

Following on from Article III, Article IV of the *Treaty* discusses partial disarmament and peaceful purposes providing that:

States Parties to the *Treaty undertake not to place in orbit around the Earth any objects carrying nuclear weapons or any other kinds of weapons of mass destruction, install such weapons on celestial bodies, or station such weapons in outer space in any other manner.* The moon and other celestial bodies shall be used by all States Parties to the *Treaty* exclusively for peaceful purposes. *The establishment of military bases, installations and fortifications, the testing of any type of weapons and the conduct of military manoeuvres on celestial bodies shall be forbidden. The use of military personnel for scientific research or for any other peaceful purposes shall not be prohibited.* The use of any equipment or facility necessary for peaceful exploration of the moon and other celestial bodies shall also not be prohibited.[32]

The first paragraph of Article IV does not bar all weapons from the Earth's orbit, from celestial bodies, or from outer space. One commentator has referred to the first paragraph as providing for a programme of 'partial disarmament'.[33] The ban on the military uses of outer space and the Earth's orbit is limited to: (1) placing in the Earth's orbit objects carrying nuclear weapons or weapons of mass destruction; (2) stationing in any manner such weapons in outer space; and (3) installing such weapons on celestial bodies. Since this provision does not ban all weapons in space, around the Earth and on celestial bodies, it can be viewed as permitting conventional, non-nuclear weapons in these zones. It is arguable that, absent a nation's expressed intent to 'place' such weapons in orbit, to 'install' such weapons on a celestial body, or to 'station' such weapons in outer space, no violation of the *Treaty* occurs.[34]

Though Article IV of the *Outer Space Treaty* provides that outer space shall be 'used exclusively for peaceful purposes', this provision while seemingly clear is also a semantic and interpretational quagmire. The impact of its ambiguity becomes clear when one considers the Reagan 'Star Wars' programme. This was the Strategic Defense Initiative (SDI) proposed by then US President Ronald Reagan on 23 March 1983.[35] The import of the initiative was to facilitate the use of *ground-based and space-based systems* to protect the US from attack by strategic nuclear ballistic missiles. It was premised on 'non-peaceful' or 'non-aggressive' uses but geared for the purpose of defending the US, a 'peaceful purpose'. Viewed in this light it means 'use' and 'purpose' acquire a strong legal connotation with the practical effect being that both military and non-military applications may be deployed for peaceful purposes anywhere in space.[36]

There has been debate on whether the use of the adjective 'exclusively' in Article IV is meaningful.[37] The word first appeared in UN General Assembly Resolution 1148 on 14 November 1957, which incorporated a proposal to develop an inspection system to ensure objects launched into space would be 'exclusively for peaceful and scientific purposes'.[38] It appears, however, that the use of the word 'purpose' in Article IV of the *Outer Space*

Treaty 'brings in the notions of both intent and of consequences; the activity must not be designed to terminate in some use of force contrary to international law'.[39] There is no indication that the *Outer Space Treaty* drafters intended the term 'purpose' to have any 'special meaning'. Thus, whether or not a 'use' was peaceful depends on its 'purpose'.[40] The term 'exclusive' merely emphasises that outer space is to be used solely for 'peaceful purposes'. Alongside the specific reference to the restriction of only particular weapons, Article IV is the setting for further controversy. It provides for two separate legal regimes for military activity in outer space: (1) activity conducted on the moon and other celestial bodies, and (2) activity conducted in outer space itself. Since Article IV divides the extra-terrestrial universe into three parts: the Earth's orbit, celestial bodies and outer space, it means then that the *Outer Space Treaty* partially frees outer space from military use. Military activity by its terms, including deployment of ASATs, is only prohibited *in toto* specifically on the moon and other celestial bodies. Outer space, as such, remains open to military activity that is non-aggressive, in line with the *UN Charter* and international law as long as such activity does not involve nuclear weapons or weapons of mass destruction. Bin Cheng notes that subject to the second paragraph of Article IV:

> nothing in Article IV(1) itself prohibits the stationing of any other type of weapons in outer space, including the moon and other celestial bodies, or in fact the use of outer space, including the moon and other celestial bodies, for military purposes in any other way.[41]

Although Article IV (2) does not prohibit the non-peaceful use of outer space away from celestial bodies; such uses are nonetheless implicitly prohibited by other provisions. For example, at least to the extent that 'non-peaceful' means the aggressive use of force, such uses are prohibited by the *UN Charter*'s provision to the contrary. A further point on Article IV relates to the legal permissibility of satellite interceptors. ASATs deviate from the non-aggressive character of virtually all other outer space and related assets, and in placement of them or other forms of deployment may appear to violate the non-aggressive mandate required of all space activities under the 'peaceful purposes' restriction. However, it is worth reflecting on Robert Ramey's observation to the effect that

> regardless of their putative 'destabilizing' character for international peace and security, the *Outer Space Treaty* does not prohibit the transiting, or even the orbiting, of conventional weaponry in space, including ASATs. The prohibition on orbiting of weapons of mass destruction, including nuclear weapons, strongly suggests the distinction between those weapons, and conventional weapons of lesser destructive power, including those directed at satellites. Though Article IV (1) could easily be modified to affect the de-weaponization of space, conventional weapons are not proscribed.[42]

From the foregoing discussion, it can be deduced that Article IV of the *Outer Space Treaty* contemplates the limited military use of space for scientific research while granting unlimited use to civilian scientific applications. However, the reality is that civilian applications of space capabilities such as weather, navigation, communications and remote sensing are equally significant for military purposes. In addition, as a technical matter, there is no bright line between military 'missiles' and civilian 'space launch vehicles.' Technologies used to build sophisticated space assets and military weaponry are often similar or even identical to the technologies required for civilian space programs.[43] The key pivot as noted by Hurewitz is premised on 'intentions, not capabilities'.[44]

Evidence that the drafters of the *Outer Space Treaty* only intended Article IV (1) to ban orbiting nuclear-type weapons is the drafters' agreement that the *Treaty* does not prohibit the stationing of land-based Inter-Continental Ballistic Missiles (ICBMs) even though their flight trajectory would take them through outer space.[45] It is well established that the only specific limitation placed on the use of the outer space void for military purposes is that found in Article IV (1).[46] Bin Cheng asserts that 'the outer void space as such can be used for any military activity that is compatible with general international law and the *Charter of the United Nations*', so long as no 'nuclear weapons or any other kind of weapons of mass destruction are stationed there.'[47]

The author now turns to consider the *Limited Test Ban Treaty*[48] whose entry into force focused only on prohibiting nuclear detonations in space. Little thought and attention seems to have been put into ensuring that the *Treaty* effectively prevented space from being turned from a sanctuary of 'peaceful' science into a battleground that may one day offer opportunities for offensive and defensive *non-nuclear* weapons. This is so since the ban focuses exclusively on nuclear weapons, meaning that other forms of weapons such as conventional, biological, chemical or high energy laser weapons can be deployed without necessarily breaching the *Treaty*. Second, to the extent that nuclear power sources operate by means other than explosion, the *Treaty* does not prohibit their use.[49]

The *Limited Test Ban Treaty*

The *Limited Test Ban Treaty* of 1963[50] prohibits nuclear weapon test explosions and any other nuclear explosions in the atmosphere, in outer space, under water and in environments in which detection is possible outside the territorial limits of the State responsible for the explosion.[51] The object and purpose of the *Treaty* are set forth in the Preamble, which states that the 'principal aim' of States Party to be

> the speediest possible achievement of an agreement on general and complete disarmament under strict international control in accordance with the objectives of the United Nations which would put an end to

the armaments race and eliminate the incentive to the production and testing of all kinds of weapons, including nuclear weapons.[52]

The Preamble concludes by stating that the intent of the States Party in entering into the *Treaty* is 'to achieve the discontinuance of all test explosions of nuclear weapons for all time' and 'to put an end to the contamination of man's environment by radioactive substances'.[53] Although the title of the *Treaty* implies that it only bans nuclear weapon tests, Article I broadens this to 'any nuclear weapon test explosion, or any other nuclear explosion' in what amounts to any place (except underground) and under any circumstances. As John Kunich notes:

> On its face, then, the [*Limited*] *Test Ban Treaty* appears to ban all nuclear explosions in space, irrespective of their peaceful purposes. Unlike the *Outer Space Treaty*, the *Treaty* is not by its terms limited to 'weapons' or to the furtherance of 'peaceful purposes'.[54]

The broad, all-inclusive language in Article I was an effort to circumvent any end-runs around a ban on nuclear weapons; but for this expansive language, some States may have tried to play games with the *Treaty* by detonating only precursors to or sub-components of nuclear weapons. When read in conjunction with the language from the Preamble, the meaning of the prohibitions in Article I takes on a different slant. The object and purpose of the *Treaty* are focused on 'disarmament' and the elimination of production and testing of 'all kinds of weapons, including nuclear weapons.'[55]

The prohibition on the use of nuclear-based explosions and propulsion is important. It essentially means that the *Treaty* bans not only nuclear arms that 'utilize atomic energy in accomplishing their intended purpose, irrespective of their size or destructive force'[56] but also weapons utilising energy forces released through the splitting or union of atoms.[57] This means that the use of fissile forces to create electromagnetic and radiation weapons with the capacity to impair electronic circuitry by the creation and/or emission of an EMP[58] or related radiation are banned as a nuclear explosion creates both. This is important as these forces in outer space can damage or neutralise the operational capability of satellites.

A significant issue is whether nuclear detonations under the *Treaty* are absolutely banned or whether they may be permissible in wartime. Egon Schwelb supports the position that the terms of the *Treaty* do permit use of nuclear weapons. Back in 1964 he stated that '[i]f [the *Outer Space Treaty*] had been intended to prohibit the use of nuclear weapons in wartime, some mention of that important purpose would certainly be found in the title and in the Preamble'.[59] This position was reiterated several years later by Dean Rusk (then US Secretary of State). In a statement to the US Senate, he asserted that the *Treaty* did not affect the US's ability to defend itself, noting that Article I (1) 'does not prohibit the use of nuclear weapons in the event of war nor restrict the exercise of the right of self-defense recognized in Article 51 of the *Charter of the United Nations*'.[60] Support of this observation is reflected in the incisive observation by Kunich that

> [a]lthough the expansive language 'or any other nuclear explosion' would on its face unambiguously ban nuclear explosions during war, even in self-defense or in a retaliatory strike, this has never been accepted as the meaning or legal effect of the *Nuclear Test Ban Treaty*. Instead, the title and the Preamble focus only on nuclear weapon tests.[61]

In any case, the position on permissibility of use of nuclear weapons in certain circumstances is still very much alive in light of the International Court of Justice's (ICJ) indecisive and non-conclusive observation regarding the issue in its *Advisory Opinion on the Legality of the Threat or Use of Nuclear Weapons*.[62]

The *Liability Convention*

The *Liability Convention on Damage Caused by Space Objects* (*Liability Convention*)[63] makes as its goal an elaboration of

> effective international rules and procedures concerning liability for damage caused by space objects and to ensure, in particular, the prompt payment under the terms of [the] Convention of a full and equitable measure of compensation to victims of such damage.[64]

Despite the provisions of the *Outer Space Treaty* prescribing the 'peaceful' use and exploration of space, the *Liability Convention* seems to recognise the distinct possibility that States may engage in intentional damage to space objects.[65] A careful reading of the *Liability Convention* discloses that the *corpus juris spatialis* implicitly recognises that under certain circumstances the intentional destruction of space objects might occur.[66]

To the extent that a hostile act in space, whether lawful or not, could harmfully interfere with a Third Party State's asset, Article IX of the *Liability Convention* appears to require that a Third State must be consulted. Further, unlike other space treaties and UN resolutions that leave the timing of such consultations unclear, Article IX specifies that it must occur before proceeding with any space activity or experiment. This could create a disincentive to carrying out activities which may involve military interference with a Third State's outer space assets as prior consultations with a Third-Party State could, by public dissemination or otherwise, constitute a *de facto* notification to the opposing belligerent State of the anticipated attack. Nonetheless, Article IX does not stand in the way of carrying through such hostile acts once 'consultations' have occurred, even if the Third-Party State objects to the anticipated activity or experiment.

Thus, the *Liability Convention* subjects States Parties to absolute liability for damage caused by its space objects on the Earth's surface, or to aircraft in flight,[67] and to liability based on fault for damage by its space object to the space object of another State 'being caused elsewhere than on the surface of the Earth'.[68] However, Ramey, in a carefully crafted and incisive insight, flags the possibility that far from the *Liability Convention* being simply a matter of claim and compensation in a classical tortious scenario, one can read into the 'with intent to cause damage' a tacit acknowledgment that in certain instances force may be used by Third States.[69]

The *Anti-Ballistic Missile Treaty*

The discussion of this specific bilateral treaty[70] may appear odd if not irrelevant to a chapter that has focused on multilateral treaties of an international nature. In any case there is a range of similar disarmament treaties in one form or another particularly between the US and the then Soviet Union carried on in contemporary times with Russia (the successor State). If one considers the *Treaty on the Limitation of Anti-Ballistic Missile Systems (ABM Treaty)*[71] as a relic of the Cold War the question would then be: what would a bilateral treaty have to do with twenty-first century problems? It is this question that this section of the book highlights and answers. Preliminarily, the importance of discussing this treaty is that it was between the two pioneering and still dominant space powers – the US and the then Soviet Union. This ensures the *Treaty*'s chequered history from the twentieth century into the twenty-first century remains relevant since the State practice of the main space faring powers was the benchmark and the *ABM Treaty*[72] contributed in fleshing out aspects of the multilateral treaties. The *Treaty* contained particularised aspects focused on prohibiting development and deployment of space-based missile defense systems and space-based mechanisms matters as noted earlier that are not specifically banned in the extant Space Law regime.[73] This section of the chapter will focus on the aspects of the *ABM Treaty*,[74] which drastically contributed to limiting the possibilities for space weaponisation in the twentieth century but were unraveled some three decades later in the twenty-first century.

The *ABM Treaty*[75] was the first non-proliferation treaty negotiated between the US and the Soviet Union during the Cold War. It served as a groundbreaking advance towards cooperation between the then two superpowers, particularly in relation to a drastic reduction of ABM arsenals and specifically for the purpose of this book – prohibitions on space-based or focused weaponry. The *Treaty* begins by recognising that limiting ABM systems would be a 'substantial factor' in curbing the arms race and would lead to a reduction in the risk of nuclear war and related delivery systems, primarily ICBMs and ABMs whose potency is enhanced by sea-based, air-based, space-based and mobile land-based ABM systems. The Mutual Assured Destruction (MAD) doctrine is based on the presumption that if each side had enough nuclear weaponry to destroy the other side then either side, if attacked, would retaliate with equal or greater force. This means neither side would rashly launch a first strike as neither would benefit from such an act. The payoff was that a tense situation may prevail, the stability created by colossal mutual loss would paradoxically maintain stability by vitiating any safety. Thus MAD sought to prevent any direct full-scale conflicts between the then superpowers and mitigate nuclear weaponry build up and associated pathways through parity by reducing arsenals to equivalent. Thus neither side should be allowed to adequately defend itself against the other's ICBMs through development of ABMs which essentially are a counter measure. The basic ethos was that ABM systems would unbalance first strike capability since it denied the Third State of the 'comfort' of strike back capacity.

The *ABM Treaty*[76] was geared specifically to solidify the MAD doctrine through two interrelated provisions – Articles I and II. Article I prohibited either of the two superpowers from deploying 'ABM systems for a defense of the territory of its country' and from 'provid[ing] a base for such a defense'.[77] The language of this provision is unequivocal – neither side may deploy an ABM system that will protect its entire territory, because that violates a fundamental tenet of MAD and would destabilise the nuclear balance. Article II of the *Treaty* places limitations on ABM systems and, more broadly, other systems. It applies to all ABM system components, including systems consisting of ABM interceptor missiles, ABM launchers and ABM radars 'deployed in an ABM role' or 'tested in an ABM mode'.[78] While it did not prevent either the US or Soviet Union (now Russia the successor State) from researching, developing or testing land-based systems, it prohibited *development, testing and deployment of sea-based, air-based, space-based, and mobile land-based ABM systems.*[79]

Similar to the analysis of 'peaceful purpose' under the *Outer Space Treaty*,[80] the issue of 'rightful intent' is important. The definitional language of Article II of the *ABM Treaty* clearly implies that intent is important, in that it defines ABM interceptor missiles, launchers, and radars as those 'constructed and deployed for an ABM role'.[81] Therefore, if any of these components were constructed and deployed for a role other than as an ABM, such as ASAT weapons, the Article III prohibition in the *ABM Treaty* would apply.

The primary provisions impacting space activity are further elaborated in Articles V and XII. The provisions tacitly recognise the legality of reconnaissance satellites as a means of verifying treaty compliance and prohibit any 'interference' with their function.[82] These provisions were no surprise since consensus was that positive activities in space included but were not limited to the use of military satellites to monitor the performance of arms-control agreements. Article V unequivocally 'prohibits developing, testing and deploying antiballistic missile systems that are sea-based, air-based, space-based, or mobile land-based.'[83] The core aspect of this *Treaty* that extends beyond its seemingly bilateral parochialism to the current arms race to aimed at weaponisation of outer space by several States is reflected by the fact that in 2001, when the US decided to withdraw from the *ABM Treaty*,[84] the debate over weaponisation not only came to the forefront but also heated up research and development – an arms race was in the making.

The withdrawal by the US from the strictures of the *ABM Treaty*[85] was geared to give it a free run in development and placement of weapon systems, which were prohibited under the *ABM Treaty* and, in particular, space-based devices which the *Treaty* banned bridging several main lacunae in the general Space Law regime. This act had a considerable impact since the *ABM Treaty* had been significant as a global stabilising force in the Cold War in seeking to attenuate and constrain general and specific activities. By the stroke of a pen the global security system was destabilised fuelling a renewed race to space weaponisation not just by Russia (the successor State to the Soviet Union) but extending to all ascendant space powers. This is more so since commencing in 2003, two years after the US withdrawal, it triggered a further seismic shift through explicit statements and formal declarations in support of space weaponisation. In 2004, USAF publicised its vision of how 'counterspace operations' could help achieve and maintain 'space superiority' and the freedom to attack through and from outer space.[86] In this regard, in the twenty-first century, since the US decision to withdraw from the *ABM Treaty*,[87] it has actively pursued innovative military technology that it considers as essential to its defence including among other initiatives to establish national missile defence shields – land-, space- and naval-based. These involve the deployment of space-based sensors, space missile tracking systems and other space-based assets which could cue ground-based interceptors.[88] Without the constraints of the *ABM Treaty*[89] that checked the then duo of major space faring powers, aspiring space powers (several and counting) are going down the weaponisation path to counter balance the US and its compliant allies. Thus, in the last several years, layered missile defense systems have reached deployment phase with practical possibilities to position interceptors in space, for example space-based kinetic energy weapons as well as Near Field Infrared Experiment (NFIRE) satellites, which can include explosive payloads.[90]

Weaponisation and militarisation of outer space revisited

As the twentieth century was coming to an end, in 1995 a study for the USAF analysing the future of air and outer space power reported that a combination of high radio frequency power and large antenna technology would allow for the projection of extremely high power densities and electromagnetic radiation.[91] The report suggested that such a weapon in GEO orbit has the capacity to create a 6 mile footprint on a battlefield, which would 'blank out' all radar receivers and damage all unprotected communication sets within that area.[92] To put the practical military dimensions into perspective one need only look at the first so called 'space war' – the 1990 Gulf War.

During the war, coalition forces were supported by 'the most sophisticated information network ever designed'.[93] Of particular significance was the role of US Navigation Satellite Timing and Ranging (NAVSTAR) GPS satellites, which enabled huge numbers of vehicles and troops to 'navigate surely across the featureless Iraqi desert' even in the middle of sandstorms and regularly surprising Iraqi forces who should have had a natural 'home advantage' over coalition troops thousands of miles from their bases and often in rather unfamiliar territory outside, for example of mock training exercises and manoeuvres.[94] GPS was also used to guide not only US air, land and air force cruise missiles and navy land-attack missiles hundreds of miles to their targets but also to generally co-ordinate operations with their seemingly variegated allies.[95] This provides an insight into the heavy reliance on technology for military effectiveness among the world's major and medium military powers. It means that outer space assets and the information based infrastructures and networks they support significantly affect not only combat readiness but effectiveness in the theatre of war.[96]

It has been noted earlier that under Article 2(4) of the *UN Charter*, States may neither use force in the course of their international relations, nor threaten it. Historically, defining what force the *Charter* prohibits given the many sources of pressure nations may use in their relations with each other has often been contentious. However, it is widely recognised that the prohibition excludes most forms of non-military physical force but encompasses certain indirect forms of military force. It is not difficult to conceive scenarios in which the use of armed force in through outer space and/or its capacities can potentially involve 'harmful interference' with other States Party given new forms of means and methods of using force.[97]

It is largely inconceivable that deployment of ASATs or satellites such as the NFIRE would be seen as a benign activity considering that they are primarily offensive in character. Thus, under the regime on the use of force, deployment of such weaponry may amount to the threat of the use of force especially where the space weaponry is hoisted and placed into proximity to another State's space assets. This is even more poignant if it occurs in circumstances where the States are on a war footing or a militarily volatile situation.

Returning to the 1995 USAF Report introduced above, the report notes that activities that threaten or have the potential to 'knock out' space assets have the potential to meet the threshold of a threat of force. Consider for example the use of space assets to jam military communication and electronic gathering facilities. To what extent can generation of 'an electronic footprint' that jams radar and other communication facilities crucial to military command systems be considered a use or threat of use of force? The matter may be considered clear-cut in the context of hostilities but is far from clear in non-hostile situations. Could a country consider the 'blanking out' of its communication systems as a tactical military strategy to test its command systems and thus a threat of use of force that would provide the basis for defensive actions say the deployment of ASATs or other related weaponry and linked flows such as generation of EMPs? These are crucial questions, more so when one considers that USSPACECOM's *Long Range Plan* encompasses with clarity the US ability to ensure uninterrupted access to outer space by its forces but also its allies by ensuring freedom of operations in outer space and an ability to deny 'hostile' Third States the ability or capacity to project or counter such operations.[98] In practical terms it implies ensuring uninterrupted access to space and maintaining an ability to deny others the use of space.[99]

Conclusion

Militarisation of outer space is a fact and its weaponisation an emerging reality. For example, in 2007 China tested an ASAT that destroyed one of its defunct satellites orbiting satellite in outer space. It was the first test of a ground-based interceptor designed to take down a satellite with the capacity to be used to carry an ASAT payload – history had been made. The following year, a US warship fired a modified tactical missile. Travelling in excess of 25,000 km an hour (more than 15 times the speed of sound) the missile hit and destroyed a malfunctioning US satellite.[100] It was the first naval interceptor to destroy a satellite in orbit – history had been remade. In both cases, despite denials by both countries that the actions were not military tests, the US and its allies on one side and China and Russia on the other continued (and continue) to trade accusations on the nature of the actions. An alarmed community expressed concern over these actions as they added greater impetus in quickening the race to space weaponisation not just by China and the US but also ascendant and aspiring space powers. The actions above are not the only issues for alarm. These are only manifestations of actions or interference with satellites having potential to neutralise operational aspects of satellites. From time to time there are incidents where satellites have been jammed by strong radio signals by blocking or reconfiguring information flows by interrupting downlink and uplink processes.[101]

Admittedly, the 'peaceful' purposes centrepiece of Space Law does not rule out the military use of outer space; however, the dynamic is different when assets are clearly of an offensive character. As space technology develops into more sophisticated areas with a variety of space-based platforms capable of carrying or launching military payloads, the issue of curbing an arms race up yonder is urgent. As early as 1986, the UN Conference on Disarmament's observation asserted that '[n]o country should develop, test or deploy space weapons in any form'.[102]

The tacit acceptance of military usages coupled with the explicit exhortations towards civilian endeavours provides a strong argument that weaponisation of space through placement of non-nuclear weapons but geared towards offensive rather than defensive purposes is antagonistic to a number of provisions of the extant outer Space Law regime as noted above. However, Richard Morgan notes that most experts agree that the *Outer Space Treaty* does not prohibit 'military use' of outer space.[103] Vlasic further notes that: '[o]uter space has achieved the dubious distinction of being the most heavily militarized environment accessible to humans'[104] since their tacit, if not explicit, acknowledgment of this reality considering that in some aspects there is strong evidence that some principles apply to the technologies meaning that 'the law of war has been incorporated into military space operations by virtue of the *Outer Space Treaty*'.[105] However, this is not black and white considering the counter perspective that space should be a science sanctuary for endeavours geared towards peace, not a battleground. This arises from the fact that provisions of the *Outer Space Treaty* and other principal instruments apply the restrictions of international law to outer space activities. Considering that the legal regime on the use of force is a product of international law, the logical presumption is that it encompasses the pacific theme that lies at the heart of the *UN Charter*.

In 2001, Hu Xiaodi – the then Chinese Ambassador on disarmament issues – warned that:

> With lethal weapons flying overhead in orbit and disrupting global strategic stability, why should people eliminate [weapons of mass destruction] or missiles on the ground? This cannot but do harm to global peace, security and stability, hence be detrimental to the fundamental interests of all States. [106]

Mark Roberts, a former UK Ministry of Defence official who was in charge of government space policy and the UK's 'offensive cyber portfolio', noted in 2013 that '[p]olicy, law and understanding of the threat to space is lagging behind the reality of what is out there'.[107] The weakness of existing treaties is seen in other activities relating to the exploitation of systems, which compromise the prohibition against space weapons thus essentially neutering the principle of 'peaceful uses' that was generally adhered to for decades, notwithstanding even the volatility of the Cold War.[108]

Although the existing *jus ad bellum* principles, which arguably apply to outer space, provide some underlying standards that regulate the utilisation of space for the purposes of armed conflict, the unique nature of outer space as a global common requires that the applicable rules be strengthened and particularised towards the environment of outer space. While some treaties seek to ban the testing, use and placement of certain types of weapons in outer space, there are many uncertainties that arise when one seeks to apply these principles to a (at this stage hypothetical) space conflict since the Space Law regime has an interpretational flexibility that exposes an internal contradiction.

When the stark reality of space warfare dawns on humankind, there will be a serious legal deficit in the absence of specific international norms restricting the deployment of weapons in outer space. The risk that space warfare will become a reality necessitates the formulation of new legal commitments by the international community. This is notwithstanding that even though the meaning of the phrase 'peaceful uses of outer space' has long defied specific definition, the dangers can be best addressed if parameters covering new technological and engineering breakthroughs are established to bypass the sometimes conflicting self-interests of space faring powers. This renews the international community's collective support regarding the principles of the use and exploitation of outer space. These goals no doubt confront very complex and traditional perceptions, but in the end represent the most secure route towards regulation.

Notes

1 Goedhuis, D. (1981) 'Some Recent Trends in the Interpretation and the Implementation of the Rules of International Space Law', *Columbia Journal of Transnational Law*, 19: 213, 226.
2 *Limited Test Ban Treaty*, opened for signature 5 August 1963, 480 UNTS 43 (entered into force 10 October 1963).
3 As noted in the Introduction to this book, militarisation and weaponisation of space have convergences and divergences. On one hand, militarisation has been around for decades since communication satellites were launched as militaries rely on satellites for command and control, communication, monitoring, early warning and navigation with GPS systems. On the other hand, weaponisation of outer space is generally understood to refer to the placement in orbit of space-based devices that have a destructive capacity. Under certain circumstances, ground-based systems designed or used to attack space-based assets also constitute space weapons.
4 Cheng, B. (1983) 'Definitional Issues in Space Law: the "Peaceful Use" of Outer Space, including the Moon and Other Celestial Bodies', *Journal of Space Law*, 11: 89; see also Richard Morgan, R. (1994) 'Military Use of Commercial Communication Satellites: A New Look at the *Outer Space Treaty* and "Peaceful Purposes"', *Journal of Air Law and Commerce*, 60: 237, 303–4.
5 For example, National Security Council Action No 1553 (21 November 1956), quoted in Paul Stares (1985) *The Militarization of Space: US Policy, 1945–1984*. Ithaca, NY: Cornell University Press, 54.
6 *Outer Space Treaty*, opened for signature 27 January 1967, 610 UNTS 205, Article IV (2) (entered into force 10 October 1967).
7 Vlasic, I. (1991) 'The Legal Aspects of Peaceful and Non-Peaceful Uses of Outer Space' in *Peaceful and Non-Peaceful Uses of Space: Problems of Definition for the Prevention of an Arms Race*, Jasani, B. (ed.), New York: Taylor & Francis, 37.
8 Ibid., 40.
9 Morgan, R. (1994) 'Military Use of Commercial Communication Satellites: A New Look at the *Outer Space Treaty* and "Peaceful Purposes"', *Journal of Air Law and Commerce*, 60: 237, 278.
10 In this regard, Nicholas Matte observes that Space Law, including the *Limited Test Ban Treaty*, *Outer Space Treaty*, *ABM Treaty* and the Moon Agreement, was developed to 'permit, indeed to endorse, the arms race, including the militarization of space'. See Matte, N. (1987) 'A Treaty for "Star Peace"' in

48 *The fourth domain: ascendance of outer space*

Matte, N. (ed.) *Arms Control and Disarmament in Outer Space: Lecture-Seminars Given at the Centre for Research of Air and Space Law*. Montreal: Centre for Research of Air and Space Law. Vol. 2, 190.

11 Ibid.
12 *Outer Space Treaty*, opened for signature 27 January 1967, 610 UNTS 205, Article IV (1) (entered into force 10 October 1967).
13 *Outer Space Treaty*, opened for signature 27 January 1967, 610 UNTS 205, Article IV (2) (entered into force 10 October 1967): 'The use of any equipment or facility necessary for peaceful exploration of the moon and other celestial bodies shall ... not be prohibited.'
14 See e.g. Kiernan, V. (1991) 'War Tests Satellites' Prowess, Military Space Systems Put to Work during Desert Storm Conflict', *Space News*, 21 January. See also John J. Meyer III (1993) 'JTF Communications: The Way Ahead', *Military Law Review*, 85.
15 Petersen, J.H. (1993) 'Info Wars', *Naval Institute Proceedings*, 119(5): 88, 96 (May).
16 Editorial (1992) 'Military Eyes CRAF-like System for Commercial Satellites', *Aerospace News*, 21 February, 285.
17 See e.g. Killette, K. (1991) 'Iraq Net Critical Target'. *Communications Week*, 21 January, 60.
18 See e.g. Perry, J.D. (2000) 'Operation Allied Force: The View from Beijing', *Aerospace Power Journal*, 14(2).
19 Jasani, B. (1987) 'Space Weapons and International Security – An Overview' in Jasani, B. (ed.) *Space Weapons and International Security*. Oxford: Oxford University Press, 19.
20 Stares, P.B. (1987) *Space and National Security*. Washington, DC: Brookings Institution, 88.
21 Collins, J.M. (1989) *Military Space Forces: The Next 50 Years*. Washington, DC: Pergamon-Brassey's, 29–30.
22 Hurwitz, B. (1994) 'Non-Proliferation and Free Access to Outer Space: The Dual-Use Dilemma of the *Outer Space Treaty* and the Missile Technology Control Regime', *High Technology Law Journal*, 9: 211, 217.
23 Statement of US Ambassador Goldberg, UN GAOR, COPUOS, Legal Subcomm, 5th sess, 62nd mtg, UN Doc A/AC.105/C.2/SR.62 (1966), reprinted in Jasentuliyana N. (ed.) (1989) *Manual of Space Law*. New York: Oceana Publications, Vol. 3, 59.
24 See e.g. Dembling, P.G. and Arons, D.M. (1967) 'The Evolution of the *Outer Space Treaty*'. *Journal of Air Law and Commerce* 33: 435.
25 Ibid.
26 *Outer Space Treaty*, opened for signature 27 January 1967, 610 UNTS 205 (entered into force 10 October 1967).
27 Ibid., Article I.
28 Ibid.
29 Ibid., Article II.
30 Ibid., Article III.
31 Ibid., emphasis added.
32 Ibid., Article IV, emphasis added.
33 Markoff, M. (1976) 'Disarmament and "Peaceful Purposes" Provisions in the 1967 *Outer Space Treaty*', *Journal of Space Law*, 3(1): 3, 4.
34 Halpern, J. (1985) 'Antisatellite Weaponry: The High Road To Destruction', *Boston University International Law Journal*, 3: 167, 181:

> whether nuclear weapons or weapons of mass destruction could be orbited around the moon or other celestial body without violating the first paragraph

of article IV, whether such weapons are permissible if they do not complete the Earth's orbit, whether for purposes of the first paragraph the moon is considered a celestial body and, if not, whether nuclear weapons and weapons of mass destruction could be installed on the moon.

35 Crowley, K. (Cold War Museum) (2008, 20 May) 'The Strategic Defense Initiative (SDI): Star Wars', [online] available at www.coldwar.org/articles/80s/sdi-starwars.asp (accessed 23 March 2014).
36 Morenoff, J. (1973) *World Peace Through Space Law*. Charlottesville, VA: Michie Company, 226.
37 See Reijnen, G.C.M. (1982) 'The Term "Peaceful" in Space Law', *Proceedings of the 25th Colloquium on the Law of Outer Space*. Paris: International Law Association, 145, 148.
38 Vlasic, I. (1991) 'The Legal Aspects of Peaceful and Non-Peaceful Uses of Outer Space' in Jasani, B. (ed.) *Peaceful and Non-Peaceful Uses of Space: Problems of Definition for the Prevention of an Arms Race*, New York: Taylor & Francis, 37, 38.
39 Fawcett, J.E.S. (1984) *Outer Space: New Challenges to Law and Policy*. Oxford: Clarendon Press, 109. See also Morenoff, J. (1973) *World Peace Through Space Law*. Charlottesville, VA: Michie Company, 296.
40 Sourbès, I. and Boyer, Y. (1999) 'Technical Aspects of Peaceful and Non-Peaceful Uses of Space' in Space' in Jasani, B. (ed.) *Peaceful and Non-Peaceful Uses of Space: Problems of Definition for the Prevention of an Arms Race*, New York: Taylor & Francis, 57, 65.
41 Cheng, B. (1983) 'Definitional Issues in Space Law: the "Peaceful Use" of Outer Space, including the Moon and other Celestial Bodies', *Journal of Space Law*, 11: 101.
42 Ramey, R. (2000) 'Armed Conflict on the Final Frontier: The Law of War in Space', *Air Force Law Review*, 1: 84.
43 Hurewitz, B. (1994) 'Non-Proliferation and Free Access to Outer Space: The Dual-Use Dilemma of the *Outer Space Treaty* and the Missile Technology Control Regime', *High Technology Law Journal*, 9: 211, 228.
44 Ibid.
45 Other weapons of mass destruction not relevant to the issue of planetary defence would be biological and chemical weapons: Gallagher, M. (1986) 'Legal Aspects of the Strategic Defense Initiative', *Military Law Review*, 111: 11, 41.
46 Cheng, B. (1997) *Studies in International Space Law*. Oxford: Clarendon Press, 529.
47 Ibid.
48 *Limited Test Ban Treaty*, opened for signature 5 August 1963, 480 UNTS 43, Article I (1)(b) (entered into force 10 October 1963).
49 Ramey, R. (2000) 'Armed Conflict on the Final Frontier: The Law of War in Space', *Air Force Law Review*, 48: 100–1.
50 *Limited Test Ban Treaty*, opened for signature 5 August 1963, 480 UNTS 43 (entered into force 10 October 1963).
51 Underground nuclear explosions are permissible if all radioactive debris is kept within the territorial limits of the State under whose jurisdiction or control the explosions are conducted: *Limited Test Ban Treaty*, opened for signature 5 August 1963, 480 UNTS 43, Article I (1)(b) (entered into force 10 October 1963).
52 *Limited Test Ban Treaty*, opened for signature 5 August 1963, 480 UNTS 43, Preamble (entered into force 10 October 1963).
53 *Limited Test Ban Treaty*, opened for signature 5 August 1963, 480 UNTS 43, Article 1 (entered into force 10 October 1963) provides:

1. Each of the Parties to this *Treaty* undertakes to prohibit, to prevent, and not to carry out any nuclear weapon test explosion, or any other nuclear explosion, at any place under its jurisdiction or control:

   a   in the atmosphere; beyond its limits, including outer space; or under water, including territorial waters or high seas; or

   b   in any other environment if such explosion causes radioactive debris to be present outside the territorial limits of the State under whose jurisdiction or control such explosion is conducted. It is understood in this connection that the provisions of this subparagraph are without prejudice to the conclusion of a treaty resulting in the permanent banning of all nuclear test explosions, including all such explosions underground, the conclusion of which, as the Parties have stated in the Preamble to this *Treaty*, they seek to achieve.

2. Each of the Parties to this *Treaty* undertakes furthermore to refrain from causing, encouraging, or in any way participating in, the carrying out of any nuclear weapon test explosion, or any other nuclear explosion, anywhere which would take place in any of the environments described, or have the effect referred to, in paragraph 1 of this Article.

54 Kunich, J. (1997) 'Planetary Defense: The Legality of Global Survival'. *Air Force Law Review*, 41: 119, 145.

55 *Limited Test Ban Treaty*, opened for signature 5 August 1963, 480 UNTS 43, Preamble (entered into force 10 October 1963).

56 Gorove, S. (1973) 'Arms Control Provisions in the *Outer Space Treaty*: A Scrutinizing Reappraisal', *Georgia Journal of International and Comparative Law*, 3: 114, 115.

57 Zedalis, R. and Wade, C. (1978) 'Anti-Satellite Weapons and the *Outer Space Treaty* of 1967'. *California Western International Law Journal*, 8: 454, 466.

58 EMP is lethal to unprotected circuitry within a very large area, harming satellites several hundred miles from the blast. Beta particles and gamma rays from nuclear explosions may also reduce the functions of space assets as they affect both radio waves and radar waves, important to the functions of satellites.

59 E. Schwelb (1964) 'The *Nuclear Test Ban Treaty* and International Law', *American Journal of International Law*, 58: 642, 644–5.

60 B. Bechhoefer, 'The *Nuclear Test Ban Treaty* in Retrospect', *Case Western Reserve Journal of International Law*, 4(13): 125, 153.

61 Kunich, J. (1997) 'Planetary Defense: The Legality of Global Survival', *Air Force Law Review*, 41: 147–8.

62 *Legality of the Threat or Use of Nuclear Weapons (Advisory Opinion)* (1996) ICJ Rep 226, 105. The ICJ noted:

   the threat or use of nuclear weapons would generally be contrary to the rules of international law applicable in armed conflict, and in particular the principles and rules of humanitarian law;

   However, in view of the current state of international law, and of the elements of fact at its disposal, the Court cannot conclude definitively whether the threat or use of nuclear weapons would be lawful or unlawful in an extreme circumstance of self-defence, in which the very survival of a State would be at stake.

63 Convention on International Liability for Damage Caused by Space Objects, opened for signature 29 March 1972, 961 UNTS 187, Article 1(b) (entered into force 1 September 1972) ('*Liability Convention*').

64 Ibid.
65 Ibid.
66 Hurewitz, B. (1994) 'Non-Proliferation and Free Access to Outer Space: The Dual-Use Dilemma of the *Outer Space Treaty* and the Missile Technology Control Regime', *High Technology Law Journal*, 9: 211, 148–50.
67 Ibid.
68 *Liability Convention*, opened for signature 29 March 1972, 961 UNTS 187, Article 3 (entered into force 1 September 1972).
69 As Ramey notes:

> Article VI provides exoneration from absolute liability in cases where either the claimant State, or the natural or juridical persons it represents, caused the damage wholly or partially by gross negligence, or an act or omission done with intent to cause damage. *A proper understanding of the phrase 'intent to cause damage' provides insight into the Convention's foresight as to the possibility of uses of force against space objects.*

Ramey, R. (2000) 'Armed Conflict on the Final Frontier: The Law of War in Space', *Air Force Law Review*, 48: 135, emphasis added.
70 See *Treaty on the Limitation of Anti-Ballistic Missile Systems*, US–USSR, 26 May 1972, 23 UST 3435. It was aimed to basically contain the nuclear arms race between the US and the then Soviet Union in various aspects including development of ballistic missile defences and reductions in the then two superpowers' strategic weapons.
71 Ibid.
72 Ibid.
73 Ibid.
74 Ibid.
75 Ibid.
76 Ibid.
77 Ibid., Article I.
78 Ibid., Article II (1) (entered into force 3 October 1972). ABM radars include target tracking and missile control radars, but not early warning radars. See 'Report of Secretary of State Rogers' (1972) *Department of State Bulletin*, 67: 3, 4.
79 See *Treaty on the Limitation of Anti-Ballistic Missile Systems*, US–USSR, 26 May 1972, 23 UST 3435, Article II (1) Article V (entered into force 3 October 1972) (emphasis added).
80 *Outer Space Treaty*, opened for signature 27 January 1967, 610 UNTS 205, Article IV (2) (entered into force 10 October 1967).
81 *Treaty on the Limitation of Anti-Ballistic Missile Systems*, US–USSR, 26 May 1972, 23 UST 3435, Article II (1), Article II (1) (entered into force 3 October 1972).
82 Ibid., Article II (1), Article XII (1)–(2).
83 Ibid. Article V (1) of the *ABM Treaty* states: 'Each party undertakes not to develop, test or deploy anti-ballistic missile systems or components which are sea-based, air-based, space-based, or mobile land based.'
84 See *Treaty on the Limitation of Anti-Ballistic Missile Systems*, US–USSR, 26 May 1972, 23 UST 3435.
85 Ibid.
86 See US Air Force (2004) 'Counterspace Operations' Air Force Doctrine Document 2-2.1, [online] available at www.fas.org/irp/doddir/usaf/afdd2_2-1.pdf (accessed 12 October 2011).

52 The fourth domain: ascendance of outer space

87 *Treaty on the Limitation of Anti-Ballistic Missile Systems*, US–USSR, 26 May 1972, 23 UST 3435.
88 Ibid. Article V (1) of the *ABM Treaty* states: 'Each party undertakes not to develop, test or deploy anti-ballistic missile systems or components which are sea-based, air-based, space-based, or mobile land based.'
89 *Treaty on the Limitation of Anti-Ballistic Missile Systems*, US–USSR, 26 May 1972, 23 UST 3435.
90 See e.g. Arms Control Association (2005) 'Action/Reaction: US Space Weaponization and China', [online] available at www.armscontrol.org (accessed 12 June 2013).
91 Bekey, I. (1995) 'Force Projection from Space' in Air Force Scientific Advisory Board, *New World Vistas: Air and Space Power for the 21st Century: Space Applications Volume*. Washington, DC: USAF Scientific Advisory Board, 83, 84.
92 Ibid., 83, 84–5.
93 Petersen, J.H. (1993) 'Info Wars', *Naval Institute Proceedings*, 119(5): 90 (May).
94 Ibid.
95 Ibid.
96 See e.g. Ramey, R. (2000) 'Armed Conflict on the Final Frontier: The Law of War in Space', *Air Force Law Review*, 48: 134.
97 Ibid., 61.
98 United States Space Command (1998) *Long Range Plan: Implementing USSPACECOM Vision for 2020*. Peterson Air Force Base, Colorado Springs, CO: US Space Command, 21.
99 Ibid.
100 See e.g. *Astronomy Magazine* (2008) 'US Successfully Destroys Satellite', 21 February, [online] available at www.astronomy.com/news-observing/news/2008/02/us%20successfully%20destroys%20satellite (accessed 14 March 2014).
101 The communication going from a satellite to ground is called downlink, and when it is going from ground to a satellite it is called uplink.
102 Conference on Disarmament, Final Record of the 350th Plenary Meeting, UN Doc CD/PV.350 (1986).
103 Morgan, R. (1994) 'Military Use of Commercial Communication Satellites: A New Look at the *Outer Space Treaty* and "Peaceful Purposes"', *Journal of Air Law and Commerce*, 60: 288.
104 Vlasic, I. (1991) 'The Legal Aspects of Peaceful and Non-Peaceful Uses of Outer Space' in Jasani, B. (ed.) *Peaceful and Non-Peaceful Uses of Space: Problems of Definition for the Prevention of an Arms Race*, New York: Taylor & Francis, 37, 51.
105 Ramey, R. (2000) 'Armed Conflict on the Final Frontier: The Law of War in Space', *Air Force Law Review*, 48: 1, 127.
106 See e.g. Arms Control Association (2005) 'Action/Reaction: US Space Weaponization and China', [online] available at www.armscontrol.org (accessed 5 August 2012).
107 Bowcott, O. (2013) 'Outer Space Demilitarisation Agreement Threatened By New Technologies', [online] available at www.theguardian.com/science/2013/sep/11/outer-space-demilitarisation-weapons-technologies (accessed 11 September 2013).
108 Ibid.

4 War in the fifth domain
Cyberwarfare

Introduction

It was noted in Chapter 2 that in 2007 Estonia experienced extensive computer hacking attacks that lasted several weeks and had the simultaneous effect of degrading and disabling key aspects of its digital ecosystem. The following year, in advance of the brief Russo-Georgian War, Georgia experienced cyber attacks similar to those suffered by Estonia in the previous year. In both cases, despite official denials, strong speculation pointed to Russian involvement. The cyber attacks highlighted the vulnerabilities generated by disruption or penetration of information and communications systems and support networks. Perhaps it was a coincidence, perhaps it was not, that a year after Estonia's cyber travails, NATO officially established the NATO Cooperative Cyber Defence Centre of Excellence (NATO CCD COE) tellingly with its headquarters in Tallinn, the capital of Estonia.[1] A year after the establishment of the NATO CCD COE the DoD announced the establishment of a Cyber Command as a subunit of Strategic Command (one of its nine combat commands).[2]

In 2009/10, a computer malware dubbed the Stuxnet worm attacked industrial Supervisory Control and Data Acquisition (SCADA) systems central to the Iranian nuclear programme. Stuxnet remains the first known worm designed to target real-world infrastructure. Its effectiveness in infiltrating an ultra-secure facility worryingly conveyed a capacity to interfere with other less secure CNI such as power stations, dams, air and ground radars. The effect of the Stuxnet in Iran's programme was to interfere with the velocity of centrifuges that enrich uranium – a critical component in civilian and military nuclear facilities. The malware in light of its capability and penetration of an ultra-secure facility is believed to have been produced by a government(s). Ralph Langner, a computer security expert, is of the strong opinion regarding the role of a State(s) in the development given the technical complexities of the worm and its specific configuration. Langner notes that:

> Code analysis makes it clear that Stuxnet is not about sending a message or providing a concept. It is about destroying its targets with utmost determination in military style ... Stuxnet is the key for a very specific

lock. In fact, there is only one lock in the world that it will open . . . *The whole attack is not at all about stealing data but about manipulation of a specific industrial process at a specific moment in time. This is not generic. It is about destroying that process.*[3]

Essentially and very significantly the worm was created solely to launch a cyber attack with the specific aim of 'destroying an industrial process in the physical world'[4] and was specifically designed to manipulate centrifugal motors with the effect that operational disruption translated into limited capacity to enrich uranium fuel. Many experts and politicians subsequently speculated on its original architects. Israel had already previously stated that cyber warfare was an important part of its national strategy and had established a military intelligence unit dedicated to this realm of engagement. Notably, in 2010 Israeli officials were coy when asked whether Israel was responsible or contributed to the creation of Stuxnet. Incidentally, prior to the discovery of Stuxnet, a US intelligence officer (attached to the US Cyber-Consequences Unit (US-CCU)) opined that a Stuxnet-like attack on centrifuges, against a State enriching uranium in violation of international treaties was legitimate. Israel coyness and lack of explicit denials by the US seemed to solidify speculations.[5] In this uncertain atmosphere and lack of explicit admission, the feeling by a good portion of the international community shifted to implicit conclusions that the 'worm' had its origins in US and Israel joint activity. While these two States were seen as the primary perpetrators there were allusions to the possibility that allies may also have rendered some form of assistance.

'One thing that differentiates Stuxnet from more run-of-the-mill malicious software is that its creators . . . incorporated lots of capabilities into it'.[6] These ranged from exploiting multiple zero-day vulnerabilities, modifying system libraries to negatively intruding on variegated mechanical and technological vectors. These capabilities meant that the 'worm' also facilitated destabilisation of Programmable Logic Controllers (PLC). This is significant since PLC systems facilitate real time output results to input conditions within specified conditions and timelines. Denaturing PLCs essentially means that precise automated and electronic processes have their multiple control inputs compromised and the operations of equipment disrupted or destroyed.

The Stuxnet incident taken together with the events in Estonia and Georgia demonstrate the ability to interfere and influence networked systems with potential to injure directly or indirectly. Cyber attacks directed against CNI such as the transport, dams and nuclear plants whose automated systems rely heavily on SCADAs can lead to widespread physical damage. This is poignant since in the 'infancy' of this new domain of intrusion/interference States are devising means and methods of attacking each other through cyber space, yet no consensus exists on the legal ramifications of when one State attacks another's computer networks. Essentially, when a sovereign State attacks another State's computer systems it falls in a grey area of crime and war: the legal and the illegal. The dilemma is: How does one filter and/or separate operationally legal acts of war, espionage and criminal acts? Without a conclusive answer to this very basic question, States will continue acting in an uncertain legal environment that leaves less timid ones unconstrained to attack others with relatively few repercussions.[7] The practicalities are that use of cyber attacks to degrade State information systems and processes exponentially amplify the likely total damage from a physical attack.[8] Would this then in relation to the extant regime on the use of force entail a formal or informal broadened interpretation of the application of Article 2(4) of the *UN Charter*'s definition on the use of force? Expanding the definition of the use of force would bring these actions within a stretched form of interpretation, but the nature of cyber attacks carries with it the danger that traditionally excluded categories on the use of force – political and economic coercion – that form a key plank of information intrusions and interferences may surreptitiously be co-opted into non-kinetic uses of force, which are generally excluded from kinetic uses of force. Jason Barkham notes that distinguishing force from economic coercion is much more difficult because the means of attack have 'some applications that traditionally are considered uses of force as well as others that typically have not been considered acts of force'.[9]

Complementing Barkham's standpoint, Erwin Dahinden observes that the traditional aim of States to achieve conventional 'equality and balance' (alluding in the author's view to military hardware – tanks, naval frigates, jets and bombs) is progressively being superseded by new strategic and tactical dimensions hinged on cyber operations available to a wide range of States.[10] Dahinden further notes (and cautions) that with 'military and technological dominance, war becomes again a politically acceptable option.'[11] This is a position that this author strongly concurs with considering that cyber attack technology is low-cost compared with conventional military hardware *and* encompasses the sort of stealth that kinetic hardware would not generally enjoy. Thus this asymmetrical dynamic means that major to medium military powers can 'even' out disparities in conventional abilities. In turn this means that States are increasingly 'less motivated to accept arms control and disarmament restrictions' as their capabilities grow and mature.[12]

Cyberattacks: classifications and analytical models

This section is a general overview of the complexities relating to the technology underpinning cyber operations. Prior developments of technology have been relatively linear such as the move from the telegraph to the telephone, radio and television, videotelephony to satellites. However, with the advent of computer networks and the Internet there was a sea-change. Computer networks and the Internet had the capability to fuse and diffuse all the forms of modern technology. The impact has been seismic positively and negatively. The complexities are such that the positive and negative aspects can be weaved together along several spectra. It is this chameleonic aspect that spawns the intricacies of non-hostile and hostile cyber operations. Since cyber attacks are a relatively new attack form, international efforts to classify them are varied owing to the dilemma posed across many fronts. This in turn means that debates on whether cyber attacks qualify as armed attacks or threats of use of force or not remain open questions in international law owing to the multifaceted landscape along which one act may be seen as hostile but in another may be seen as non-hostile. This uncertainty has lead scholars and commentators to reflect and articulate classifications and analytical models that provide beacons on the various parameters in dealing with these unconventional activities. Such classifications and models are relevant to cyber attacks because activities often straddle different dimensions.

The outline in this section of the chapter on some of the main positions seeks to provide a guide to the various complexities operationally and thus the different impacts on the application on the use of force regime. The aim is to account for the variegated landscape encapsulated in the analysis of hostile cyber operations across several legal and operational spectrums (sometimes independently, in parallel or simultaneously). There are a number of convergent and divergent models that have a practical operational military bearing on several modalities of ascendant and emerging aspects of IW. In the next paragraphs, this section will outline and engage with some of the key perspectives. The author's caveat is that the snapshots are not inclusive of all models/analytical frameworks but rather a general overview to reveal different extant classifications that account for the undulating terminology and perceptions relating to cyber warfare across the board, from experts and commentators to militaries and scholars. This means that despite some definite aspects, there are no bright-line distinctions.

The colours of cyber interruptions and disruptions

Michael Schmitt distinguishes between Information Operations (IO) and IW. He notes that information operations are 'any non-consensual actions intended to discover, alter, destroy, disrupt or transfer data stored in a computer manipulated by a computer or transmitted through a computer network'.[13] This may be offensive CNA, military deception, psychological operations, electronic warfare, physical attack and special information operations or defensive.[14] It is noted that IW is generally conducted during times of crisis or conflict to achieve or promote specific objectives over a specific adversary or adversaries.

Martin Libicki and Nigel Duncan base their classification in relation to information warfare according to type or method, rather than purpose. They describe seven forms: electronic warfare; command and control warfare; psychological warfare; intelligence based warfare; economic information warfare; hacker warfare; and cyberwar fare.[15] In what the author considers a model that expands on the position of Libicki and Duncan, Michael Sklerov in a crisp enunciation outlines three models and general parameters regarding 'non-conventional attacks' through three holistic spectra.

a) Model I: an *instrument-based approach* based on whether the damage caused by a new attack method could only have been previously achieved with a kinetic attack.
b) Model II: an *effects-based approach* in which the attack's similarity to a kinetic attack is irrelevant and the focus shifts to the overall effect that the cyber attack has on a victim State.
c) Model III: a *strict liability approach*, in which cyber attacks against CNI are automatically treated as armed attacks, due to the severe consequences that can result from disabling information systems and processes.[16]

The US DoD in a more encompassing enunciation that takes largely into account the various perspectives above divides the aspects of cyber-space into specific spectra along physical and non-physical information infrastructure and processes with a three-layered approach:

1 *Geographic component:* the physical location of elements of the network that covers the note that even in cyber space and boundless boundaries there is still a physical aspect tied to other domains.
2 *Physical network component:* hardware and infrastructure that supports networks and physical connectors.
3 *Logical component:* network aspects linked to the connections that exist between network nodes.

Having set out the variegated aspects of cyber space across which hostile and non-hostile activities can occur, the chapter turns to a particularised focus on the interplay of the use of force regime amidst these complexities. The outline of different analytical and classification models enables an appreciation of the too often turns and twists in legal analysis in juxtaposing cyber space to legal indicia.

Cyber conflict along the spectrum of armed attack

Cyber operations are generally not kinetic in nature (though they can produce kinetic effects. Generally they do not employ what would in common parlance would be considered as 'weapons' since the regime on the use of force as noted in Chapter 1 is focused on devices designed or used for inflicting bodily harm or physical damage. Arguably this extends to gaining military advantage or defence but as noted earlier this second aspect is not explicitly captured in the definition of armed attack.

Smokeless warfare: worms, viruses and trojans

The harmful basis of hostile cyber operations is malicious software (malware). There are different variations and configurations of malware. At a rudimentary level these consist of two broad classes: 'worms' or 'viruses'. These basic definitions will suffice. A worm is an independent program that copies itself onto other computers but usually does not change other programs.[17] On the other hand, a virus essentially has a code fragment that attaches itself to a program and operates when its host begins to run software. Worms can cause damage merely by clogging/consuming bandwidth. Viruses on the other hand are self-replicating and enmesh themselves into an operating system(s). They have the capacity to access information and thus the ability to cause theft, loss or corruption data or crashing hard disks.

At first glance hostile cyber intrusions would appear not to be 'armed attacks' given the variance with kinetic actions. However, cyber operations can have destructive physical results even though intrusions are not physically violent in themselves as they can generate harmful consequences (physical and non-physical). To the extent that they result in injury or death of persons or damage or destruction of property, the attacks may satisfy the armed attack threshold. For consideration would be whether the 'sublime' penetration of the power centrifuges by the Stuxnet worm against the Iranian nuclear power plants (if a State was behind this) would meet the general threshold since physical damage was a consequence. As the International Group of Experts that crafted *Tallinn Manual on the International Law Applicable to Cyber Warfare* (*Tallinn Manual*) noted '[t]he clearest cases are those cyber operations, such as the employment of the Stuxnet worm, that amount to a use of force. Such operations are also facts on intervention because all uses of force are coercive *per se*'.[18] This brings to light spectrums on the higher end of the digital infiltration relating to specific military pathways which encompass deployments (of an offensive nature) of elements such as High-powered Microwaves (HPM) encompassing Electromagnetic Pulse Bombs (E-bombs) and Microwave Amplification by Stimulated Emission of Radiation (Maser). These devices in different ways produce power – the sort of power that may be used to affect the opposing side's perception of reality or to destroy or to damage its infrastructure and may lead to exertion of military pressure or an increased risk from traditional war.[19]

What distinguishes a cyber attack from other cyber provocations is pegged on the variegated consequential effects. The follow up technical and also legal question is what effects are sufficient to trigger self-defence in circumstances where there is material and/or human harm? In a considered view, Nicholas Tsagourias notes:

> it is important to recall the circumstances under which self-defence can be exercised. These are prescribed in Article 51 of the *UN Charter* and in the customary international law of self-defence. Both branches of the

law seem to agree that what triggers the right to self-defence is an armed attack . . . *a cyber attack that causes substantial human and/or material destruction can be equated to an armed attack for purposes of self-defence . . . for example, when a cyber attack on an air traffic control system, or a cyber attack on a nuclear reactor, caused substantial material or human destruction.*[20]

The observation above is echoed by the *Tallin Manual*, which notes that '[c]yber operations in which the cause and effect are clearly linked are more likely to be characterized as uses of force'.[21]

Information warfare: colliding or colluding with the regime on the use of force?

Article 51 of the *UN Charter* by its dictates seems to exclude at basic interpretational level cyber warfare since it was not the type of hostile operation that was in the minds of the founders of the UN or the international community then. As noted in Chapter 1, the term 'armed attack' strongly indicates that a response to aggression can only be justified after a kinetic attack thus only an armed ('conventional') attack can trigger a defensive action, not other forms of coercion or intrusions. In this regard, guidance as to use of force is garnered from the concomitant discussion than a species of non-kinetic attack – economic sanctions or related coercive measures. In this regard, States led by Brazil proposed to extend the ambit of Article 2(4) to non-kinetic coercion, particularly economic.[22] The proposal was resoundingly defeated by a vote of 26–2, indicating that the *Charter*'s authors were primarily concerned with kinetic attacks.[23] This means then that based on the intent of the *Charter*'s authors seeking to embrace cyber warfare within the *UN Charter*'s use of force and parameters of Article 2(4) and Article 51 would lead to an opposite interpretation.[24]

It may be averred that mitigatory leeway can be anchored in Article 2(3), which lays out another core *UN Charter* basic principle entailing that '[a]ll Members shall settle their international disputes by peaceful means in such a manner that international peace and security, and justice, are not endangered'.[25] Its import is that the intention of the *UN Charter*'s authors was to end not only 'armed conflict' but also *anything that might challenge 'peace and security'*.[26] A cyber attack could easily threaten peace and security when one considers the importance of CNI in modern society. Since the maintenance of the 'peace and security' is a central purpose of the UN, any form of activity that threatens this (including cyberwarfare) could arguably fall under the umbrella of Article 2(4), which prohibits use or threat of force against the territorial integrity of a State.[27] Territorial integrity could be interpreted in many ways, such as whether a State's territorial integrity includes its cyber space. Coupled to this is the reminder that under Article 39 of the *UN Charter*, the Security Council is granted wide ranging legal and political power to 'determine the existence of any threat to the peace, breach of the peace, or act of aggression' against a State, and to take steps to restore the 'peace and security'.[28] This power then potentially adds a number of other activities besides the explicitly listed and particularised provisions encapsulated in the relevant Articles of the *UN Charter*.

Physical destruction: is data property?

By 2012, twelve States acknowledged active development of defensive *and* offensive cyber capabilities.[29] These developments are not simply confined to a handful of the major powers but stretch further with some three dozen medium, ascendant and emerging powers on the same trajectory and the number can only rise. Many States now have specific units in their defence ministries and/or militaries dedicated to all aspects of cyber operations. On this note one need only consider the reality that since the turn of the twenty-first century statist-based cyber attacks have been rising in frequency *and* aggressiveness. A couple of examples suffice outside of the usual exchanges between established major global powers. The breadth of cyber operations in different continua encompasses States at different levels of military capability and hegemonical aspirations based as noted on the asymmetric aspects, since they traverse the length and breadth of CNI (civilian and military) yet deliver significant blows to a States daily affairs even in peacetime.

A couple of examples illustrate the response quandary. In 2012, the Saudi Arabian national Oil Company (ARAMCO) – the world's largest producer of oil – had its SCADAs and other information processes attacked. It is estimated that essential data on thousands of hard drives were destroyed.[30] To mitigate the damage and the destabilising effect (considering that in excess of 85 per cent of its revenues are derived from and based on this resource), an emergency shut down of oil related activities (ranging from extraction to domestic consumption and export) was put in effect. The flow on effect was not simply confined to its national economy but globally in view of the centrality of oil. It is strongly suspected that Iran was behind this operation for a whole host of reasons, not least the aspiration of the two countries on a number of premises including regional hegemonic ambitions and 'containment'.

In 2013, another tinderbox was to manifest itself on the other side of the world by actions in the Korean Peninsula – one of the world's most militarised zones – which triggered significant global unease. South Korea's CNI was penetrated through hostile cyber operations (primarily its banking and financial infrastructure). It was to cost South Korea's economy hundreds of millions of dollars in direct and indirect costs.[31] Fingers pointed to its neighbour and traditional foe – North Korea. As States waited with bated breath attributability, despite strong suspicion, was not conclusive. Unpacked munitions triggered by the episode were reluctantly packed away. These two seemingly peripheral episodes by medium (emergent) military powers give a glimpse of the regional dangers that may arise but with ramifications for international peace and security. On this note the author reflects, in a journalistic term: What would be the result if major established powers 'drew their guns'?

Cybersnooping: unrefined frontier

The possibilities of legitimately accessing a system may appear suspicious but could be an inadvertent event – information systems and processes do malfunction in unpredictable ways as opposed to kinetic forms; missiles do not launch themselves and neither do tanks self-drive and fire at specific targets. If a State were to respond automatically to the apprehension of a seemingly hostile incursion by counter-attacking, adverse consequences may arise, this on one hand owing to the attributability problem already identified and on the other the chameleonic nature of mapping specific electronic pathways owing to the civilian/military diffusion inherent in information networks. However, countering cyber intrusions effectively often means using methods that are layered with offensive capabilities. If the penetration causes little damage on a Third State(s) then a minimalist counter-attack may leave room for diplomatic intercession that may avoid an escalation. In any case from a hard-nosed legal view based on minimalist reaction the affected State(s) may not have an automatic right to take defensive action since the intrusion would be equated to a minor border breach and the armed attack indicia potentially not met. This said, given the layered nature of electronic intrusions the actual full-scale attack might still be pending. As Jason Barkham notes:

> The severity of an IW attack cannot be identified readily, so it would not be feasible to require a victim to conduct a damage assessment to determine whether an IW penetration were a use of force or merely of coercion. More importantly, while an intrusion might have been detected, the full extent of the attack might not be known for some time. IW attacks that are acts of force cannot be distinguished readily from those that are not.[32]

Large-scale attacks are technically easier to assess and quantify providing leeway in co-relating them to 'conventional' methods of warfare. This would sit comfortably within traditional use of force analysis. However, low-level hostile intrusions are problematic when juxtaposed with Article 2(4) of the *UN Charter*. As Barkham notes '. . . [t]hey cannot be analyzed readily under Article 2(4) because they threaten to erase the distinction between acts of force and acts of coercion'.[33] This dynamic is underpinned by the practical reality that digital infiltrations may not give leeway for assessment and thus potential quantification when the activity may be surreptitious access to commercial data rather military oriented acts. Thus attacks that undermine the value of data create considerable problems for Article 2(4)'s use of force analysis than attacks that actually destroy data. Unlike attacks that destroy property, acts of subversion, which could include interfering with satellites, stock market manipulation, denial of service attacks and industrial espionage, could rob the property of its value without causing any actual physical damage.[34] Under Article 2(4) of the *UN Charter*'s traditional analysis there would be no weapon used and no property destroyed, so the act would not rank as a use of force, since cyber intrusions generally target and manipulate data. It is in this regard that a significant dilemma arises: Can data be considered property and thus its destruction or manipulation be analogised to a use of force?

Though the data might be whole afterwards, the networks and CNI it supports would have been degraded. A reflection in this trajectory is Chapter 3's analysis regarding manipulating a Third State's satellite into a different orbit. The satellite itself would not be damaged since the action interferes only with the positioning. However, it negates the Third State's ability to receive satellite imagery or other information which is specific to military utility such as interlinkages of command and control systems, reconnaissance and surveillance particularly relating to a hostile environment or assessment of the nature of a military mobilisation, or simply confirming whether a missile launch is simply a test or a targeted action. Thus in this scenario, even though there is no kinetic impact or any physical damage to property valuable information is at stake. Applying more liberal interpretations of the prohibition against force, a finding of the use of force on the grounds that the security provided by a specific information network or process may be impaired, the attacker might be using the victim State's 'electronic/digital blindness' to act elsewhere. However, up pops the fact that espionage is generally legitimate, but here the peacetime/wartime dilemma identified elsewhere in this book arises. The quantitative and qualitative quandaries discussed in this section of the chapter are addressed in the *Tallinn Manual*, which notes that:

> a cyber operation that can be evaluated in very specific terms (e.g. amount of data corrupted, percentage of servers disabled, number of confidential files exilfrated) is more likely to be characterized as a use of force than one with difficult to measure or subjective consequences.[35]

Electronic blockades: new perception or old shackles

Traditionally, military 'blockades' or 'quarantines' have involved air or naval interdictions, which aim to delay, disrupt or destroy enemy forces and supply lines, thus pre-emptively emasculating the capacity of opponents to do any harm. These have from time to time been undertaken in modern times often by unilateral actions and mixed reactions by the international community. Often condemnation may be voiced but occasionally there is quiet acquiescence. However, UN mandated sanctions are legitimate and are within the mandate of the UN Security Council. This is provided for under Articles 41 and 42 of the *UN Charter*. These Articles respectively cover kinetic and non-kinetic actions:

> Article 41: The Security Council may decide what measures not involving the use of armed force are to be employed to give effect to its decisions ... These may include *complete or partial interruption of economic relations and of rail, sea, air, postal, telegraphic, radio, and other means of communication* ...[36]
>
> Article 42: Should the Security Council consider that measures provided for in Article 41 would be inadequate or have proved to be inadequate ... *Such action may include demonstrations, blockade, and other operations by air, sea, or land* forces of Members of the United Nations.[37]

Use of unilateral measures as mentioned above outside a UN mandate remains controversial with the baseline being that they are generally not readily accepted even when the measures are characterised as defensive in character. The key reason is that the use of force by a State through naval or air interdiction is traditionally seen as falling on the continuum of use of force, which is prohibited. In relation to cyber intrusions the actions against Estonia and Georgia are emblematic. Their digital ecosystems were largely disabled/disrupted in what could amount to an 'electronic blockade', which in an era of reliance on information networks and processes to manage CNI does arguably generate effects of traditional naval or air blockades, albeit this time establishing a ring of electronic suffocation. Does this amount to a threat or use of force? There are two major problems caused by not defining 'electronic blockades' as a threat or use of force. This would make them legitimate under international law as by their dynamic they would fall outside of the scope of Article 2(4) read together with Article 51. This said, Barkham is of the opinion that in certain circumstances an electronic blockade would fall within the definition on use force on the basis that if

> the embargo were to shut down the target State's information systems by disabling its servers or by a denial of service attack, that seemingly would be a use of force, since the act would take place within the opposing party's systems and, by extension, its territory. Even if the embargo were accomplished by blocking data transmission before it reached the routers within the target State, this would be analogous to a naval blockade, which is a use of force.[38]

It is arguable that large-scale electronic blockades fall within the regime on the use of force. The difficulty arises in relation to small-scale hostile intrusions, which generally do not bear the intense and protracted velocity of large-scale attacks since they are often manifested in discrete isolated incidents. This means that small-scale hostile intrusions can and do exploit the gap between Articles 2(4) and 51 considering that limited means of prevention do not translate well to cyber space where there are no borders to mark the point when preventative measures may be undertaken. The layered nature of attacks often means that drawing bright line distinctions between the components of defines and offense is a legal and practical nightmare. It may well be that an act of self-defence slips into the landscape of reprisals which violate international law. Further, it may well be that counter activity may probably fall within the realm of retaliation. The *Tallinn Manual* notes:

> acts falling into these and other such categories are presumptively legal (although in a particular situation they may in fact violate an international norm). This being so, they are less likely to be considered by States as uses of force.[39]

Small-scale or large-scale attacks: reflections on quantitative evaluation

Article 2(4) of the *UN Charter* prohibits intervention that violates the territory of a State. However, it does not explicitly (and arguably implicitly) allude to '. . . more subtle forms of 'subversive' coercion. . . .'[40] Christopher Joyner and Catherine Lotrionte note that '[t]he line separating unlawful intervention from legitimate interference is often difficult to draw'.[41] As they note in elaborating this standpoint, it is 'easy to argue that incursions by military forces across national borders violate international norms', but as already noted in various parts of the book and in particular the genesis of the *UN Charter* and subsequent developments and perspectives of the international community '. . . mere economic and diplomatic forms of coercion are more likely to fall within the realm of permissive behaviour'.[42] This position by Joyner and Lotrionte is one that the author is in firm agreement with. This said, the quandaries relating to non-kinetic action/intrusions still persist on account of their novelty as pathways of military operations. The challenge remains distinguishing the subtlety of digital interferences and to what extent and how they can be analogised to the extant regime on the use of force given the various permutations and combinations of activity. Transnational operations do not necessarily trigger legal implications in light of the prohibitions encapsulated in Article 2(4).[43] But reiterating sentiments expressed above, qualitative *and* quantitative assessments still create a fog on what incursions constitute force or the use of force since the baseline is that the *UN Charter* is by and large fixated on unlawful violence threatened or committed against persons and/or property.

Can an act of cyber warfare trigger an international response based on the definition of use of force? On one hand, the use of force prohibition generally evolves around kinetic armed attacks, leaving cyber warfare largely uncovered by the *UN Charter*. On the other hand, considering more broadly the entirety of the *Charter*'s fundamental purpose of protecting peace and security globally, any activity that intrudes on this exhortation ought to be penalised. The *Tallinn Manual* notes that '[a] cyber operation constitutes use of force when its scale and effect are comparable to non-cyber operations rising to the level of a use of force.'[44] There are of course thresholds on the use of force as noted in Chapter 1 and elsewhere in this chapter and cyber operations by virtue of their mostly non-kinetic nature will continually test the *UN Charter* regime on the use of force.

Several decades ago, Iain Brownlie exploring the use of force averred that Article 2(4) includes force besides 'armed force' but did not explicitly specify the nature of these other potential applications of force.[45] Canvassing this hanging matter, the author is of the opinion (albeit delicate) that cyber incursions with injurious physical impact on a State's CNI would comfortably meet the threshold. How about the scenarios where incursions destabilise and interrupt CNI infrastructure with no *immediate* animate or non-animate material damage? While physical destruction may not occur, unavailability of particularised purposes could produce harmful or coercive effects. Dispensing (temporarily) with cyber actions that do not produce kinetic effects: Do hostile activities fit within extant prohibitions? How can the practical and legal loop be closed in light of the fact that cyber activities can be varied in *time, scope* and *effect*? Do Distributed Denial of Service (DDoS) attacks (considering that the aim is to make network resources and/or processes unavailable) against a foreign State's digital ecosystem breach the legal rule prohibiting use of force? Is a DDoS action an act of coercion that fits within the ambit of acts prohibited by the *UN Charter*? Does a State's intentional interference with or interruption of another State's digital ecosystem violate international legal rules? Would such interference be sufficiently coercive so as to amount to a breach of the international standard that prohibits the use of force?[46] This section concludes with the position of the *Tallinn Manual* with its allusion of the fact that the ICJ in the *Nicaragua Case* opined that 'intervention is wrongful when it uses methods of coercion' with the caveat 'that cyber espionage and cyber exploitation operations lacking a coercive element do not *per se* violate the non-intervention principle.'[47]

Specific targeting of military facilities: any difference

This section seeks to build on the discussion above. The author considers that this sub-section on its own is apt since the dynamics above encompass in varying degrees the interlocking of civilian and military pathways, which will always be present. However, this sub-section in a snapshot focuses specifically on particularised CNI relating to military activities. It explores whether specific and focused cyber intrusions targeted solely on military facilities fall within the thresholds of the regime on use of force. The big question is whether a cyber attack specifically targeting a State's military ecosystem produces a specific certainty that overrides *per se* the general response dilemma.

Arguably specific attacks on military facilities would more easily satisfy the self-defence criteria in situations of significant degradation of military oriented CNI results. This takes two spectrums – physical and non-physical. The physical aspect where material damage to infrastructure and/or human harm is inflicted through kinetic force is generally seen as straightforward within the realm of the use of force. However, it is arguable that in certain conditions it extends to where consequences are not manifested materially but result in massive disruption; for example, disabling or destabilising a State's command and control systems – seen as non-kinetic.

The issue for reflection is whether such disruptions to military oriented infrastructure can be analogised and thus linearly (in a legalistic sense) and effectively breach the indicia related to an armed attack; the pivot being that activities that neutralise or immobilise military information networks and processes are *per se* hostile in nature since such intrusions may be a prelude to a kinetic attack. Is self-defence triggered? The complexity still remains regarding qualitative and quantitative assessment and whether such penetration would indicate that it is part of an overall attack. The fact that digital infiltrations will regularly pose the major dilemma of attributability as they can (and often are) multi-layered since the malicious infiltration of the system, the execution of the payload and the production of the harmful effects may take place in different time frames.[48] As the *Tallinn Manual* notes: '[w]hereas the immediacy factor focuses on the temporal aspect of the consequences . . . directness examines the chain of causation'.[49] Tsaugourias fleshes this out with his observation that 'an attack would exist from the moment the harmful effects materialize irrespective of when the system has been infiltrated or the payload has been executed'.[50] The practical issue identified by Tsaugorias is the fact whether a State that becomes aware 'that its systems have been compromised . . . can take passive or active cyber defence measures to neutralize the threat'.[51] This author agrees with this reflection but differ with Tsagourias on the spectrum relating to the allusion that a 'State can resort to pre-emptive self-defence if all other means of neutralizing the cyber threat fail'.[52] This is on the basis that the author considers that this position, while operationally practical and linear, crosses the contested and often abused threshold of pre-emption, which has largely never gained significant legal traction owing to the fact that too often States have abused this and instead of explicit acknowledgement they have sort to craft dubious legal justifications pegged on aspects of self-defence.

Conclusion

The right to self-defence has limitations since not all uses of force qualify as armed attacks. As the ICJ noted in the *Nicaragua Case* governments do not perforce have the right of armed response to acts that fall short of constituting an armed attack. Only military attacks, and not every isolated armed incident, rise to the level of an armed attack.[53] However, Malcolm Shaw addresses the controversial aspect of the case by noting that the ICJ adopted a *de minimis* approach to armed attack since 'an attack may assume different dimensions in the light of the political or psychological circumstances of the moment. What in one context may seem relatively insignificant, may in others assume considerable importance prompting the need to respond in self-defence'.[54]

Certain acts of intrusions may be unlawful, but that fact does not necessarily give a State the right to respond by using armed force in self-defence. Louis Henkin put it well when he observed that the UN 'recognise[s] the exception of self-defence in emergency, but limit[s] [it] to actual armed attack, which is clear, unambiguous, subject to proof, and not easily open to misinterpretation or fabrication'.[55] Despite the *Nicaragua Case*[56] confirming that an armed attack can in specific circumstances take an indirect form, some commentators argue that a State need not wait to be attacked before the right to defend its territorial integrity can be exercised. In any case the *UN Charter* is not a 'suicide pact'. This then means that the notion of pre-emptive or anticipatory self-defence remains on the table in the event of imminent danger or an actual threat of armed attack. The legal caveat is that the threat must be real and credible with a genuine probability of attack. Gauging this conclusively can often be illusive and trigger an overreaction that crosses the line between legality and illegality. Harking back to the *Caroline Incident*, the standard set then (and tacitly acknowledged in contemporary times) is that a threat must be '*instant, overwhelming, leaving no choice of means, and no moment for deliberation*'.[57] Thus if a State is under continuous, foreign-instigated, hostile intrusions and is suffering physical, financial or other harm, the State is not expected to tolerate events that are destroying its CNI. It seems reasonable that a government subjected to such operations will be inclined to respond immediately. However, a response crisis is ever present based on the often multi-layered nature of infiltrations. Suppose the harmful effects of an intrusion materialise several weeks after a hostile act that cripples core CNI. Is a State granted a right of action since the time lag may well mean any counter initiatives may be considered to fall within the realm of reprisal or retaliation?

In sum, cyber space as the fifth domain of battle space is in tension with many basic aspects of international law governing the use of force. Existing attempts at defining cyber warfare within the current *jus ad bellum* paradigm fail to offer adequate clarity on response partly because the technology inherent in cyber warfare makes it difficult to attribute the attack to a specific source or to characterise the intent behind it, since acts of cyber warfare can occur separately but on a similar platform, together but in parallel, simultaneously but not immediate.

Notes

1 Detailed Information on NATO Cooperative Cyber Defence Centre of Excellence (NATO CCD COE) is available from its official website www.ccdcoe.org (accessed 1 August 2012).
2 Details of the process and background details leading to the establishment of the US Cyber Command and its activation can be found in an Article by Garamone, J. (2010) 'Alexander Details US Cyber Command Gains', *American Forces Press Service*, 24 September, [online] available at www.defense.gov/news/newsarticle.aspx?id=61014 (accessed 12 January 2014).
3 Moore, M.S. (2010) 'War With Iran? Stuxnet May Be First Cybersalvo', *Christian Science Monitor*, 28 September, [online] available at www.psmag.com/navigation/politics-and-law/war-with-iran-stuxnet-may-be-first-cybersalvo-23321/ (accessed 4 April 2014) (emphasis added).
4 Ibid.
5 See e.g. Mueller, P. and Babak Yadegari, B. 'The Stuxnet Worm', [online] available at www.cs.arizona.edu/~collberg/Teaching/466-566/2012/Resources/presentations/2012/topic9-final/report.pdf (accessed 3 February 2013).
6 Ibid.
7 Friesen, T.L. (2009) 'Resolving Tomorrow's Conflicts Today: How New Developments within the UN Security Council Can Be Used to Combat Cyberwarfare', *Naval Law Review*, 58: 89, 91.
8 Sklerov, M.J. (2009) 'Solving the Dilemma of State Responses to Cyberattacks: A Justification for the Use of Active Defenses Against States Who Neglect Their Duty to Prevent', *Military Law Review*, 201: 1, 21.
9 Barkham, J. (2001) 'Information Warfare and International Law on the Use of Force', *New York University Journal of International Law and Politics*, 34(1): 57, 59.
10 Dahinden, E. (2005) 'The Future of Arms Control Law: Towards a New Regulatory Approach and New Regulatory Techniques', *Journal of Conflict and Security Law*, 263, 269.
11 Ibid.
12 Ibid.
13 Schmitt, M. (1999) 'Computer Network Attack and the Use of Force in International Law: Thoughts on a Normative Framework', *Columbia Journal of Transnational Law,* 37: 885, 891.
14 Ibid. See also Haslam, E. (2000) 'Information Warfare: Technological Changes and International Law', *Journal of Conflict and Security Law*, 5(2): 157, 161–2, who addresses the spectrums articulated by Michael Schmitt.
15 Libicki, M. and Duncan, N. (1998) 'A Primer on the Employment of Non-Lethal Weapons'. *Naval Law Review*, 45: 1, 7–8.
16 Sklerov, M.J. (2009) 'Solving the Dilemma of State Responses to Cyberattacks: A Justification for the Use of Active Defenses Against States Who Neglect Their Duty to Prevent', *Military Law Review*, 201: 1, 54–5.
17 See Denning, D.E. (1999) *Information Warfare and Security*. Essex: Addison-Wesley Longman Ltd, 280–1.
18 Schmitt, M.N. (ed.) (2013) *Tallinn Manual on the International Law Applicable to Cyber Warfare*. Cambridge: Cambridge University Press, 45.

19 Feaver, P. (1998) 'Blowback: Information Warfare and the Dynamics of Coercion', *Security Studies*, 7: 92.
20 Tsagourias, N. (2012) 'Cyber Attacks, Self-Defence and the Problem of Attribution', *Journal of Conflict and Security Law*, 17(2): 229, 230–1 (emphasis added).
21 Schmitt, M.N. (ed.) (2013) *Tallinn Manual on the International Law Applicable to Cyber Warfare*. Cambridge: Cambridge University Press, 49.
22 See e.g. G.A. Res. 3314 (XXIX), UN Doc. A/9732 (Dec. 14, 1974); Charter, 26 June 1945, 59 Stat. 1031, 892 UNTS 119, Preamble; Elagab, O.Y. (1992) 'Economic Measures against Developing Countries', *International and Comparative Law Quarterly*, 41(3), 682, 688.
23 Ibid.
24 *UN Charter*, 26 June 1945, 59 Stat. 1031, 892 UNTS 119, Preamble.
25 *UN Charter*, 26 June 1945, 59 Stat. 1031, 892 UNTS 119, Article 2(3).
26 Ibid. (emphasis added).
27 *UN Charter*, 26 June 1945, 59 Stat. 1031, 892 UNTS 119, Article 2(4).
28 Ibid., Article 39.
29 See e.g. Lewis, J.A. (2013) 'On the Offensive in the Cyberspace Arms Race', *The Washington Post*, 13 October, [online] available at www.japantimes.co.jp/news/2013/10/13/business/on-the-offensive-in-the-cyberspace-arms-race/#.U05G3W DjiM8 (accessed 1 April 2014).
30 Ibid.
31 Ibid.
32 Barkham, J. (2001) 'Information Warfare and International Law on the Use of Force', *New York University Journal of International Law and Politics*, 34(1): 57, 111–12.
33 Ibid., 57, 111.
34 Ibid., 57, 89.
35 Schmitt, M.N. (ed.) (2013) *Tallinn Manual on the International Law Applicable to Cyber Warfare*. Cambridge: Cambridge University Press, 51.
36 *UN Charter*, 26 June 1945, 59 Stat. 1031, 892 UNTS 119, Article 41 (emphasis added).
37 Ibid., Article 42 (emphasis added).
38 Barkham, J. (2001) 'Information Warfare and International Law on the Use of Force', *New York University Journal of International Law and Politics*, 34(1): 57, 92.
39 Schmitt, M.N. (ed.) (2013) *Tallinn Manual on the International Law Applicable to Cyber Warfare*. Cambridge: Cambridge University Press, 51
40 Joyner, C.C. and Lotrionte, C. (2001) 'Information Warfare as International Coercion: Elements of a Legal Framework', *European Journal of International Law*, 12(5): 825, 846.
41 Ibid., 825, 848.
42 Ibid.
43 Ibid., 825, 848–9.
44 Schmitt, M.N. (ed.) (2013) *Tallinn Manual on the International Law Applicable to Cyber Warfare*. Cambridge: Cambridge University Press, 45.
45 Brownlie, I. (1963) *International Law and the Use of Force by States*. Oxford: Oxford University Press, 265–78.
46 These rhetorical and practical questions are constructed from the analysis of Joyner, C.C. and Lotrionte, C. (2001) 'Information Warfare as International Coercion: Elements of a Legal Framework', *European Journal of International Law*, 12(5): 825, 849. These rhetorical questions do not purport to reflect the analysis but acknowledge that the discussion was the basis of the inspiration.

47 Schmitt, M.N. (ed.) (2013) *Tallinn Manual on the International Law Applicable to Cyber Warfare*. Cambridge: Cambridge University Press, 44.
48 Tsagourias, N. (2012) 'Cyber Attacks, Self-Defence and the Problem of Attribution', *Journal of Conflict and Security Law*, 17(2): 229, 230–1.
49 Schmitt, M.N. (ed.) (2013) *Tallinn Manual on the International Law Applicable to Cyber Warfare*. Cambridge: Cambridge University Press, 49.
50 Tsagourias, N. (2012) 'Cyber Attacks, Self-Defence and the Problem of Attribution', *Journal of Conflict and Security Law*, 17(2): 229, 232.
51 Ibid.
52 Ibid.
53 See *Military and Paramilitary Activities In and Against Nicaragua (Nicaragua v. US)*, ICJ Reports (1986) 1, 93–9.
54 Shaw, M. (2014) 'Principles of International Law on the Use of Force by States in Self-Defence', *Working Paper, ILP WP 05/0*, [online], 17–18, available at www.chathamhouse.org/publications/papers/view/108106 (accessed 23 April 2014).
55 Henkin, L. (1979, 2nd edn) *How Nations Behave*. New York; Columbia University Press, 142.
56 See *Military and Paramilitary Activities In and Against Nicaragua (Nicaragua v. US)*, ICJ Reports (1986) 1, 93–9.
57 See *The Caroline Case*, in Moore, J.B. (1906) *Digest of International Law* (Vol. 2). Washington, DC: US Government Print Office, 409 (emphasis added).

5 Discarding law by analogy
Old legal frameworks for new threats

Introduction

International law does possess some significant principles that bear relevance to the complexities of the information RMA discussed in previous chapters. However, the international law framework does not broadly provide many particularistic principles and doctrines that can readily accommodate extant and emerging information technologies and platforms. This means that specific aspects of threats to digital ecosystems and commons often have to be analogised in light of the fact that in contemporary times technological innovations have matured much faster than existing regimes and thus present challenges to a range of fundamental tenets of international law. In this regard, Sean Kanuk notes that:

> Today, public international law faces perhaps its greatest challenge as information technology transforms international society. Just as territorial boundaries and natural resources formed the theoretical foundation for an international legal paradigm in an age of geopolitical borders, so too must a conceptual framework based on information under gird the legal institutions of the twenty-first century.[1]

In a rudimentary reflection by the author, engineering and technological advances validate 'Moore's Law' with its prediction that over the history of computing capacity doubles approximately every two years.[2] While this seems to be related to particular aspects of computing, it is precisely such rapidity that is reflected in technological change across information systems, processes and capacities. The ever increasing efficiency and power of digital devices has transformed outer and cyber space into formidable assets for better or worse depending on the intended purpose. As noted in previous chapters, digital uses by States raise a number of legal and technical challenges based on the asymmetry of high gain, low risk. Varied practice of States regarding offensive and defensive strategies means that there are different conceptions and conceptualisations on the precise nature of hostile non-kinetic activities.

72 Discarding law by analogy

In this concluding chapter, the author seeks to set out modalities through which some of the contested aspects regarding militarisation of the digital commons (outer and cyber space) may be addressed through extant international legal frameworks either through specific principles or analogy. The suggestions may be modest, but based on the realities that particularistic treaties focused on the digital commons or revisions of extant frameworks they are unlikely to happen in the short term (and probably the medium term). This means that the next best thing in the interim is using extant norms of international law as potential paradigms to de-escalate the increasing technological and digital arms race. In some ways the suggestions for outer space and cyber space may seem artificial, but do have practical substance in articulating specific paradigms informed by extant doctrines and principles.

Outer space: addressing a clear and present danger

Resolving the 'peaceful purposes' conundrum: disengaging legal shadows from operational substance

The *Outer Space Treaty* as mentioned amounts to the 'Constitution' of outer space. It was the first treaty to not only set rules governing access to space, but more pertinently addresses the issue of space militarisation and weaponisation, at least to a certain degree. The fundamental premises of the *Outer Space Treaty* are that outer space is not open to national appropriation but reserved for the pursuit of peaceful purposes in the common interest of mankind. In the process of banning the placement of Weapons of Mass Destruction (WMD) in orbit and the banning of offensive military oriented assets, the *Outer Space Treaty* enshrines the concept of peaceful use of outer space. However, as discussed in Chapter 3 of this book, there still remain differing opinions on the operational definition of 'peaceful'. Among many States, the term 'peaceful' has become synonymous with the term 'non-aggressive' rather than 'non-military'. This implies that military uses are allowed and lawful as long as they remain 'non-aggressive' as permitted under Article 2(4) of the *UN Charter*.[3]

The fundamental premise of the *Outer Space Treaty* is that this global common is not open to national appropriation but reserved for the pursuit of the common interest of mankind. The underlying goal was (and remains) to avoid the 'colonisation' of this global common.[4] At that time, due to the minuscule number of States capable of operating in outer space, in the early years the *Outer Space Treaty* was largely untested and weaponisation mostly seen as a non-starter owing to the engineering and technological hurdles. Consequently, the international community largely accommodated military support activities such as observation, surveillance, communications and the detection of nuclear explosions on Earth, since these were seen as 'passive' and thus falling under the umbrella of 'peaceful purposes'.[5] However, the engineering and technological hurdles were surmounted much faster than expected and the major space powers increasingly saw outer space as a military platform that offered many advantages in active military operations. In this regard, Andrew Park notes:

> While all hope for preserving space for peaceful purposes is not lost, [there is a need to] narrow the definition of peaceful purposes if progress is to be achieved. The era of space as a truly peaceful sanctuary may be gone, but it may not be too late to regulate space activities in an effort to mitigate the potential of space weaponization.[6]

It is significant that for decades many national and international statements have gravitated towards prevention of an arms race in outer space by affirming and re-affirming that outer space should be used for peaceful purposes, not for military advantage. For example, the various UN Conferences on Disarmament, the General Assembly, the Committee on the Peaceful Uses of Outer Space (COPUOS) and the international scientific community use this phrase as a basis for deliberations. Space-based weapon systems are not consistent with a norm, which binds space faring nations by conventional law but also arguably principles that have aggregated from soft law to international custom. In any case, the *Vienna Convention on the Law of Treaties*[7] provides that a State that does not act in good faith disregards *pacta sunt servanda* and thus violates extant treaty commitments. Back in 1985, Martin Feinreider cautioned that international lawyers reviewing treaties and State practice 'must ascertain fairly the parties' intentions and the resulting legal obligations, and then analyze subsequent practice with a view to furthering good faith performance of such obligations'.[8] He further warned that it is not appropriate to 'rely on strained readings of text and disingenuous presentations of fact to erode legal obligations and thus rationalize avoidance of constraints on State behaviour'.[9]

The caution by Feinreider is particularly relevant to one of the central provisions of the *Outer Space Treaty* – Article III, which provides that States shall carry out activities in space in accordance with international law, including the *UN Charter*, in the interest of maintaining international peace and security. In essence then, the question of maintaining international peace and security should preclude utilising space as a medium of warfare. The only possible exception would be a defensive system, but this is clearly a rather slippery slope. In any case no State would feel the need to field a defensive system in space when no space weapons are deployed by other States. This means then that the best paradigm would be a blanket proscription of any deployment of weapons in outer space as well as land or sea based military assets that can penetrate outer space.

The position on a blanket proscription of weapons deployment in space is buttressed by a couple of poignant illustrations. To commence with one of the major space faring powers, the Soviet Union (now Russia) has argued

74 *Discarding law by analogy*

in the past and maintains the position that it is important that outer space be excluded from the sphere of the arms race and that all channels for militarisation and weaponisation of outer space be blocked. As early as 1981, the Soviet Union submitted to the UN Committee on Disarmament a *Draft Treaty on the Stationing of Weapons of any Kind in Outer Space.*[10] The *Draft Treaty* sought to ban deployment of all types of weapons in outer space and to provide for the use of technical monitoring facilities to this end. Little headway was made leading the Soviet Union two years later to once again make specific proposals on banning and eliminating space attack weapons. The main elements of this second initiative were:

1 The prohibition of the testing or deployment by placing in orbit around the Earth or stationing on celestial bodies or in any other manner of any space-based weapons for destruction of objects on the Earth, in the atmosphere or in outer space.
2 The prohibition of the use of space objects in orbit around the Earth, on celestial bodies or stationed in outer space in any other manner as means to destroy any targets on the Earth, in the atmosphere or in outer space.
3 The obligation of States not to destroy, damage, or disturb the normal functioning or change the flight trajectory of space objects of other States.
4 The prohibition of the testing or creation of new anti-satellite systems and the destruction of such systems that may already exist.
5 The prohibition of the testing or use of manned space craft for military, including anti-satellite, purposes.
6 The provision for a broad range of measures to verify compliance with the obligations envisaged by the *Treaty*.[11]

In 1984, during the 39th Session of the UN General Assembly, the Soviet Union once again tabled a proposal whose underpinning philosophy was that the General Assembly should proclaim that the historic responsibility of all States is to ensure that exploration of outer space should be carried out exclusively for peaceful purposes and for the benefit of mankind.[12] The Soviet proposal proposed that the UN General Assembly declare that the exclusion of outer space from the sphere of the arms race is an international obligation, and that the prevention of militarisation would provide an opportunity for the peaceful use of space to solve the acute economic, social and cultural development problems facing mankind. The UN General Assembly took this on board noting that there was a grave concern regarding the extension of an arms race into outer space and opined that the conclusion of a treaty to safeguard international peace and security was a worthwhile venture.[13]

However, one needs to consider that among some States the position is that peaceful use of space depends on the purpose of the activity.[14] This would mean that the arguments against the militarisation and weaponisation of outer space are rendered redundant since the argument by space faring nations is that their programs are geared towards advancing national self-defence – a 'peaceful purpose'. Further traction for this argument is to be found in Robert Ramey's synthesis of State practice. He notes that an examination of the Space Law regime discloses that, at a minimum, the following military activities in outer space are not prohibited:

1 the use of military personnel;
2 the use of space-based remote sensors in support of combat or other military purposes;
3 the use of space-based communication, navigation, and meteorological systems for combat or other military purposes;
4 the deployment and non-aggressive use of conventional space weapons; and
5 the transiting of nuclear and other weapons of mass destruction in non-orbital trajectories.[15]

Despite the loopholes identified the reality remains firmly that Space Law requires that 'outer space' be used for 'peaceful purposes'. This doctrine is an accepted axiom and continues to be recognised in the majority of space-related international agreements and UN declarations or resolutions enacted to date. This is buttressed by the *UN Charter*'s exhortation that requires States to maintain peace in the interests of international security. Equally, the *Outer Space Treaty* explicitly confirms that this requirement is applicable to outer space as asserted by the UN Conference on Disarmament in 1986. It noted that outer space should be used exclusively for peaceful purposes for the benefit of '... mankind. No country should develop, test or deploy space weapons in any form. An international agreement on the complete prohibition of space weapons should be concluded through negotiations as soon as possible.'[16] Although it has its shortcomings, the *Outer Space Treaty* has, for the most part, withstood the duration of time, and for that exact reason, an effort to strengthen it is worth pursuing with an amendment to the *Outer Space Treaty* to specifically prohibit deployment of military assets in space that have distinct aspects of weaponisation. The author enthusiastically supports this position since it would generate a great deal of valuable momentum.[17] The most substantial barrier to an amendment is likely to be the reluctance of States to accept new limitations upon their sovereign autonomy to use force in space. However, the momentum for these positions exists since key space faring nations have espoused positions and proposals that aim to achieve a complete demilitarisation of outer space.

In 2000, the Chinese Ambassador to the UN Committee on Disarmament voiced his country's view that '[t]he prevention of an arms race and the prohibition of weapon systems in outer space will . . . exempt outer space from wars . . . [and will] be crucial for maintaining peace, security, and

76 *Discarding law by analogy*

stability on the Earth'.[18] Further in sentiments seemingly targeted at the US, the Ambassador went on to note that 'attempts to seek so-called 'absolute superiority' for oneself at the expense of the security of others will definitely go nowhere and benefit nobody'.[19] Subsequently in 2001, Russia, which ostensibly shares the same stance as China, initiated and hosted an international conference addressing the avenues to prevent an arms race in outer space.[20] Two years after the conference, China publicly declared 'that space should not be militarized and that space technologies should be used for peaceful purposes'.[21] This is even more poignant when one considers that it was in the same year that an ascendant China joined the 'Space Club' after successfully launching a manned space flight becoming only the third State in the history to do so.

In 2006, some two decades after the initial 1984 proposal (by the Soviet Union) urging the conclusion of a treaty explicitly banning and eliminating space attack weapons, Russia (the successor State) argued that if all States observed a prohibition on space weaponisation it would vitiate an arms race. Russia (with China's support) asserted that an obligation of no use or threat of use of force against space objects was not only practical but sensible. Once again, submission of a draft treaty to this end was tabled at UN regarding placement of weapons in outer space.

In light of the above positions and assertions of the main space faring States, which broadly have the support of other States, there seems to be a gathering momentum both in letter and spirit for an agreement being reached on the prohibition and elimination of space weaponry and all other systems designed to destroy objects in space. The future of space security will depend greatly on how quickly but also effectively this initiative is attained.

Re-orientating the peace and security framework

One of the most profound events at the start of the twenty-first century in regard to international peace and security was the devastating terrorist attacks on 11 September 2001 against the US. The horrors of September 11 and the events that unfolded on that tragic day presented a terrible day in history.[22] While this attack marked the maturation of global terrorism, its ramifications were far wider; the attacks pointed to the fact that drastic events outside of the contemplation of the *UN Charter*'s drafters would change the international security environment. This was manifest in President George Bush Jr's speech in June 2002 to the 200th graduating class of the US Military Academy at West Point. In his speech, Bush Jr noted that:

> The gravest danger to freedom lies at the crossroads of radicalism and technology. When the spread of chemical and biological and nuclear weapons, along with ballistic missile technology – when that occurs, even weak States and small groups could attain a catastrophic power to strike great nations.[23]

Though the West Point speech was focused largely on the maturation of global terrorism, the author will dwell on a theme that was rather poignant – the dangers of proliferation of technology. While Bush Jr dwelt on the matter of advanced technology being in the hands of terrorists, it is also just as important that States themselves avoid developing space weaponisation technology that will inevitably lead the international community down the path of insecurity and ignite an arms race. While it would seem as strange for the author to use the West Point speech as a platform to argue against space weaponisation, it is imperative that a few factors are brought to light. First, the history of mankind would be hard pressed to judge States kindly – States have proved to be just as irresponsible as non-statal entities in the use of armaments. Second, new technology has only served to open new avenues for efficient killing whether that be use of atomic devices in World War II, landmines or cluster bombs. Lastly, the nature of State hegemonic competition has always been dominated by a belief that economic and political power is underwritten by military might.

In the international arena, any threat to global security is a problem shared by all members of the UN, particularly when new technology points to development of devastating space weaponry. The deadlier the technology and likelihood of military conflagration, the more concrete international debate is required. In this respect, it is important to recall that the UN security system addresses both form and substance. Indeed, the *UN Charter* does not prohibit the use of force, but it does seek to regulate its use. The more sophisticated and complicated forms of using military forces under international auspices require the UN to contribute to the shaping of both the practice and scope of the international disarmament agenda with regard to space. What greater curative platform would there be than dealing with threats that have the potential of widespread deadly effects but that have not yet materialised? Some five decades ago, John Kennedy (then US President) asserted during the 1962 Cuban Missile Crisis that: 'We no longer live in a world where only the actual firing of weapons represents a sufficient challenge to a nation's security to constitute maximum peril.'[24] This twentieth-century statement rings true today in the twenty-first century. It is to be remembered that the sophist justification for the Soviet initiative to place nuclear weapons/components in Cuba was that it was a reaction to a US-initiated arms race (and vice versa) that necessitated proximity.

The author argues strongly that there is no way argument can be made (logically or otherwise) that maintaining international peace and stability is served by ratcheting up an arms race in outer space and the correlative danger of the use of armed force. There is a need for the UN to carry out a re-appraisal of its regime on the use of force and re-interpret it in a different light. We no longer live in an era when the most powerful weapons were muzzle-loading cannons with a maximum range of about 3 miles! The nature of space weaponry as outlined in Chapter 3 is such that there is great leeway for military confrontation to emanate from a misunderstanding such as a malfunctioning laser that 'blinds' a Third State's satellite or a satellite being hoisted into orbit that accidentally detonates creating a deadly Van Allen Belt field,[25] which disables Third State's space assets whether military or civilian. Who will prevent or counsel the victim State that it was not a sneak 'Space Pearl Harbour' when space faring powers are getting anxious about the vulnerability of their space assets?

The author argues that the existence of the UN as a quasi-universal international institution has fundamentally changed the character of the international system and the post-World War II international security system. This is based on the reality that despite a number of failings the *UN Charter* has shown itself adept in adapting to a variety of new tasks, but this remains incomplete. While the *UN Charter* system as a means to restrain the use of force has developed more fully than the *Charter* system's ability to authorise and to enable States to use force against a member State, Article 1 remains pivotal to the *UN Charter*'s mandate. This Article articulates the central purpose of the UN to ensure effective collective measures for the prevention and removal of threats to the peace, and for the suppression of acts of aggression.[26]

There is no doubt that the UN was founded to be attentive first and foremost to peaceful settlement of international disputes and to rely on the military solutions *only* as an extreme last resort.[27] The Security Council is thus required to fulfil a central constitutive principle of the UN, stated in the *Charter*'s stirring preamble: 'to save succeeding generations from the scourge of war.'[28] The undercurrent is a recognition that the *UN Charter* provision, though crafted in an age before the advent of intercontinental ballistic missiles, WMDs and space weapons, nonetheless offers room to accommodate a mandate that addresses the weaponisation of space. In this regard, the UN should seize the chance before rather than after space powers deploy weapons in outer space. This may well afford a platform for a moratorium on deployment of weapons in outer space and a window of opportunity to negotiate a total ban of weapons in outer space.

Coercive arms control

Article 39 of the *UN Charter* grants wide discretionary power to the Security Council. This arguably is supported by the fact that the drafters of the *Charter* did not offer precise definitions as to what constitutes a 'threat to the peace', a 'breach of the peace' or an 'act of aggression'. Although the General Assembly eventually reached a rather limited definition of aggression, the Security Council is not bound by it.[29] Given the history of the Security Council, the reality is that the scope of these terms are fluid and could well embrace the emerging space arms race by providing the Security Council a platform to classify certain activities in space as 'acts of aggression'. This would enable the regulation of deployment by space faring powers of devices that are obviously geared to be offensive.

Arms control policy and strategy, perceived as a programme and framework in which the international community shares common objectives, can be achieved on a basis of shared expectation and agreements. This will serve the international community by providing greater strength and public security. In this vein, it may be the time to dust off some of the ideas encompassed by previous initiatives. For example, in 1957, Western States, including the US, proposed the creation of an 'inspection system which would ensure the use of outer space exclusively for peaceful and scientific purposes'.[30] About three decades later in 1985, as the realisation dawned that the US had leapt significantly ahead in the development of space weaponry technology, the then Soviet Union proposed the creation of a 'World Space Organization', which would ensure 'international cooperation in the peaceful uses of outer space in the context of its non-militarisation'.[31] These initiatives ought not to be viewed as simplistic pipe dreams, but rather as the basis for serious propositions that may well afford the international community the opportunity to re-engage in serious deliberations to address and contain the matter of space weaponisation.

Speaking at the 2010 UN Disarmament and International Security Committee meeting, the Russian representative Victor Vasiliev noted that the prevention of the placement of weapons in outer space remained one of the foreign policy priorities of his country.[32] He went on to note that in 2008 at the Conference on Disarmament, together with China it had put forward a draft international treaty, out of a 'deep understanding that it was easier to ban now the placement of weapons in outer space than to sort out a weapon mess some time later'.[33] Vasiliev concluded by noting that preventing the appearance of weapons in outer space was extremely important from the point of view of assuring predictability of the strategic situation in outer space, global stability and safety and security in general.

The International Environmental Law Platform

After several decades of State activity in outer space, the amount of debris – macro and micro particulate matter – already pose very significant hazards to space assets. Outer space orbits – LEO, GEO and SSO – are essential for both civilian and military systems. Despite the broad expanse of outer space, only particular orbits can be used meaning that satellite orbits are a *finite natural resource*. A major and very significant handicap of the outer space environment is that it has little ability to rid itself of debris. It is thus a particularly delicate and fragile environment owing to its lack of capacity to repair itself.[34] Only the Earth's atmosphere can remove satellites from orbit when the sun flares up in its eleven-year cycle and heats the upper atmosphere and makes it expand so that debris and spacecraft in low orbits are subjected to increased drag.[35] But this is only of limited utility as it applies only to LEO. With objects in GEO and SSO being in higher altitude there is less air, hence reducing the ability for drag and thus potential ejection of debris.[36]

80 *Discarding law by analogy*

This means that debris orbiting approximately 800 km above the Earth resulting from testing, deployment and use of space assets (whether satellites or weapons) reside there for decades.[37] Disturbingly, once debris settles into orbit at more than 1,500 km above Earth's surface, it remains there indefinitely, continuously orbiting Earth at up to 17,000 mph.[38] With current technology, computer models can only track space objects in LEO that are over 10 cm in diameter and objects in GEO that are over 1 m in diameter. Only about 8,500 objects are currently trackable and the number is unlikely to rise exponentially given for once the limitations in technology in monitoring micro-particulate matter. This is of particular worry given that estimates show that up to 3,500,000 untrackable objects reside in space and are cascading and increasing day in day out.[39]

Outer space is already under considerable strain from the demands of the numerous services it has to support. These range from meteorology, GPS systems and environmental monitoring to surveillance and to communication services that ensure safety of life in land, air and sea. Deploying space-based weapons in the increasingly crowded orbits will limit other activities. More significantly, weaponisation of outer space and the various modes of how the devices work stand to generate more space debris and increase the population of debilitating matter exponentially. Speaking in 2010, Ambassador Laura Kennedy, the then US Permanent Representative to the Conference on Disarmament, noted that: 'The interconnected nature of space capabilities and the world's growing dependence on them mean[s] that irresponsible space acts could have damaging consequences for all.'[40] She further noted the grim reality that decades of unbridled space activity have already significantly littered the Earth's orbit with debris and the physical danger to space assets posed by increasing activities in space.[41] Thus weaponisation could only serve to compound the outer space environment crisis since: 'If a number of satellites were to be destroyed during the course of a war ... they would create so much debris that it would prevent future satellites from being stationed in space and generally limit space access.'[42]

Many experts and commentators state that, even if mankind launched no new objects into orbit, the debris population would continue to increase exponentially and make at least parts of Earth orbit, such as LEO, unusable.[43] The matter is sufficiently serious that as early as the 1990s the topic of space debris was placed on the full UN COPUOS agenda out of concern for inability and eventually the technological challenges to remove known debris. Marietta Benkö notes that:

> problems resulting from the production of space debris do not only affect the (growing) number of space-faring nations, but also every single country and its inhabitants. Everyday life world-wide depends significantly on space services. Let me just mention: phone, fax and online

banking as well as the use of the internet as a source of communication and information ... Therefore civilians and the military have the same interest in keeping outer space 'clean' which makes the rational and prudent use of this environment an imperative in order to preserve its uses also for future generations.[44]

Scholars note that deliberate use of kinetic and hypervelocity weapons in space in the course of a war could potentially create a battlefield that would last forever, potentially encasing the entire planet in a shell of whizzing debris that will thereafter make space near the Earth highly hazardous for peaceful as well as military purposes.[45] This is owing to the 'cascade effect' – an uncontrollable process by which space debris continuously self-generates.[46] The more space objects there are in orbit, the greater the probability that there will be a collision. With each new collision there is a corresponding increase in the amount of debris, which would then result in an even greater probability of collisions.[47] As Benkö cautions:

> it is established that [space debris] do not only pose a risk to space activities in the orbit where they were generated. For example, if an Earth orbit is polluted by a debris cloud (which is always spreading rapidly *i.a.* through the uncontrolled collision of the debris pieces with each other as well as explosions as a result of such collisions) access from the Earth to outer space can be in serious danger if space objects have to cross this orbit upon launch or re-entry. As a result such an orbit can have the effect of 'barbed wire' around the Earth.[48]

The international community has generally approached the space weapons issue solely in terms of arms control. COPUOS has long recognised that weaponising space undermines both non-proliferation efforts and the notion of maintaining outer space for peaceful purposes. However, it is to be noted that the US has often hobbled wide ranging and concrete initiatives within the wider UN system through efforts to ensure that disarmament issues remain only within the mandate of the UN Conference on Disarmament (CD). This in turn severely limits the scope of COPUOS's debates and defined initiatives despite Chinese and Russian overtures for a treaty.[49] It is of note though that Lori Scheetz firmly asserts that:

> [e]mploying an international environmental framework, the international community can address issues outside of traditional national security interests, such as the obligations of the present generation to prevent destruction of the space commons resulting from the development or use of space weapons.[50]

It is to be recalled that Article VI of the *Outer Space Treaty* provides that State Parties shall bear international responsibility for national activities in outer space, regardless of whether or not those activities are conducted by government or private entities.[51] This provision of the *Treaty* arguably applies to space debris because it results from States' activities in outer space. However, in terms of prevention of debris, as opposed to responsibility for debris, the provision is not adequate. Thus, Article VII of the *Outer Space Treaty* extends the tenor of Article VI by dealing more specifically with liability of a State for damage to another State which is a party to the *Treaty*, from the other State's space object or its components.[52] While this might serve to deter some States from producing debris, the weakness of the provision is that it does not expressly prohibit the creation of space debris. In this regard, Edward Finch notes:

> The existing treaties make no reference to the protection of the space environment as an area separate from provisions dealing with its use. Although their provisions could be interpreted to encompass the problem of space debris, solution through mere interpretation is not possible. The international community must take bolder and more concrete measures.[53]

Following on from the discussion above, the *Registration Convention* among other issues provides that: 'When a space object is launched into Earth orbit or beyond, the launching State shall register the space object by means of an entry into an appropriate registry.'[54] Article II legally binds States to inform the UN Secretary General of entries into the registry.[55] Article II(1), requires a launching State of a space object that is launched into Earth orbit, or beyond, to register such space object by means of an entry in an appropriate registry, which it shall maintain and inform the Secretary General of the UN of the establishment of such a registry.[56] This provision arguably ensures that the international community is kept aware of which State is responsible for which space object and enables the UN to observe outer space activities of States. Bolstering this is Article VI, which makes it an obligation of all State Parties, particularly those that possess space monitoring and tracking facilities to render assistance in identifying a space object that causes damage to other space objects or persons.[57] This provision would ensure the identification of parties responsible for specific activities in outer space and thus make it easier to impose liability for environmental damage caused by its space object.

This author concludes with the observation that since outer space is the common heritage of all mankind, all States have an obligation regarding development and enshrinement of policies and objectives of any entity affecting outer space regardless of their level of involvement in space. Further sustainable development in the context of the outer space environmental avenue entails banning space weapons when one considers intergenerational equity.[58]

Cyber space: act now not later

Refocusing on the principle of non-intervention

Traditionally, legal appraisal of interventions in the domestic affairs of States has been approached from the use of force perspective.[59] As the ICJ noted in the *Nicaragua Case*, the use of force is a 'particularly obvious example' of an unlawful intervention.[60] However, as Robert Jennings and Arthur Watt note, while customary rules of international law relating to intervention are to a considerable extent 'considered alongside the more general prohibition on the use of force, intervention is still a distinct concept'.[61] Christopher Joyner and Catherine Lotrionte, in a statement that encompasses the viewpoint of Robert Jennings and Arthur Watts, articulate that:

> [t]he line separating unlawful intervention from legitimate interference is often difficult to draw. It is easy to argue that incursions by military forces across national borders violate international norms, and that mere economic and diplomatic forms of coercion are more likely to fall within the realm of permissive behaviour. The dilemma becomes apparent, however, when attempts are made to distinguish between more subtle kinds of intervention, such as naval interdiction, massive economic sanctions, humanitarian intervention, and computer-directed forms of cyber-assault.[62]

Cyber intrusions as noted elsewhere in the book are not *per se* an armed attack, considering the dynamics of kinetic (physical) force and non-kinetic (non-physical) force. However, digital intrusions of various forms whether large-scale or small-scale fall broadly in the realm of interference of a State's sovereignty since there remains a trans-boundary aspect to digital and electronic data flows. Russell Buchan commenting on the utility of the doctrine of interference as a bridge that aligns kinetic and non-kinetic activity notes that:

> [i]n examining the legality of cyber attacks many commentators have focused exclusively on Article 2(4), failing to consider the wider customary principle of non-intervention. Whilst others have recognized the potential application of this principle, they mention it only very briefly; crucially, these authors do not engage in a sustained analysis of how the non-intervention principle may apply to cyber attacks, particularly those falling below the threshold of an unlawful use of force.[63]

A conclusive multilateral framework?

In the 1990s, as the concept of cyber warfare first began to receive widespread attention, there were some efforts within the international community

84 *Discarding law by analogy*

to negotiate an agreement.[64] In 1998, Russia tabled a resolution in the UN's First Committee (whose remit is Disarmament and International Security) in an effort to get the UN to focus strongly on the subject.[65] The resolution included a call for States to collectively move towards a formal ban the development, production and use of particularly dangerous information weapons.[66] However, the initiative received unenthusiastic support among major military powers, which arguably curtailed its journey to consideration at a UN General Assembly plenary. The following year, the US DoD produced a document that examined the range of treaties and international law that might pertain to the conduct of cyber warfare. The assessment concluded first, that the international community is unlikely to promptly produce a coherent body of law on the subject.[67] Second, no clear legal remedies exist to address cyber warfare operations.[68] Third, the document recommended analysing the various elements and circumstances of any particular planned operation or activity to determine the applicability of existing international legal principles.[69]

Currently, a number of existing international treaties contain norms relating to telecommunications that potentially inform cyber intrusions. However, these are generally tangential with regard to offensive cyber intrusions. For a start, the *International Telecommunications Convention* (*ITC*) prohibits harmful interference with telecommunications.[70] Under the provisions of Article 12(2)(f) the International Telecommunications Union (ITU) is mandated to:

> assist in the resolution of cases of harmful interference, at the request of one or more of the interested administrations, and where necessary, make investigations and prepare, for consideration by the Board, a report including draft recommendations to the administrations concerned.[71]

Article 12(4) of the *ITC*, however, largely negates the operational aspects of Article 12(2)(f) by affirming that the Convention's main focus is radio channels. It does acknowledge that 'in those portions of the spectrum where harmful interference may occur', there is need for equitable, effective and economical use of satellites and their orbits, but once again this is along the continuum of the ITU's primary focus – radio channels. Essentially then, the effectiveness of the treaty is limited by this exception, even if by casuistry it may be argued that its norms analogise to cyber spaces and thus a potential viable regulatory platform. Moving on to the 1989 Agreement on the Prevention of Dangerous Military Activities signed by the US and the then Soviet Union; this instrument prohibits harmful interference with enemy command and control systems, therefore seeming to suggest norms that could designate digital attacks. However, once again this would (in the author's opinion) be a stretch of a treaty that was specific and focusing on particular issues without the flexibility often afforded or read into declarations.[72]

Rethinking legal thresholds for information warfare

No provision of modern international law explicitly prohibits IW because of the tacit acceptance that certain digital and electronic intrusions in situations of hostility, such as jamming and spoofing orbital assets, are permissible. The crux of the matter is in undeclared hostilities or peacetime intrusions. What international law does not prohibit it generally permits. However, the absence of a prohibition against IW is not dispositive, since general principles of international law may pose constraints as they do regarding 'traditional' modes of warfare. Does this leave wiggle room for regulating the use of the variegated uses of IW techniques? The quagmire is that in a number of situations it is difficult to gauge indicators of hostile intent and thus co-relation to the use of force regime.

International legal rules and State practice presently support actions in self-defence. Does this also include attacks on national information infrastructure? A government's response to a cyber attack, like that to any force, must comply with the prescribed legal principles set down in the concepts of necessity, imminence and proportionality. This means that the intent behind a cyber attack should be taken into account in making decisions. Certain factors serve as useful guidelines when considering whether to act in self-defence, among them the following:

1. a clear indication of intent by the offending State;
2. the availability and sufficiency of evidence to demonstrate that preparations for the attack have advanced to the point where it is imminent; and
3. the ability to make the advantage of a pre-emptive attack proportional to the risks of precipitating a war that might otherwise be avoided.[73]

Deciding whether a particular form of cyber-based attack meets the conditions of necessity and imminence depends on perceptions of the threatened State. Joyner and Lotrionte note:

> A targeted government's decision to respond also depends on that State's vulnerabilities and the potential for damage by a particular cyber attack. Similarly, the perceived intent of the offending government may determine the level of response by a target State. If the government of a targeted State believes that another State's assault on its information systems merely serves as a prelude to a larger conventional attack, then it might view the 'non-armed' assault as the first phase in a war-making process.[74]

Conclusion

It falls to be determined whether IW constitutes an unlawful use of force or an armed attack justifying self-defence according to Articles 2(4) and 51 of the *UN Charter*.[75] This may already reflect the view of some States. It has been claimed that the effect of an information attack is similar to that of the use of WMDs, hence from a military point of view the use of IW means should be considered a non-military phase of a conflict, whether there is damage and/or casualties. This chapter concludes with Emily Haslam's call for '. . . a new international legal paradigm to identify non armed intervention as aggression, since 'directed violence of any sort within the international community whether against individual property or information is not compatible with the international public order'.[76]

Notes

1. Kanuck, S.P. (1996) 'Recent Development, Information Warfare: New Challenges for Public International Law', *Harvard International Law Journal*, 37(1): 272, 274.
2. See e.g. Moore, G.E. (1965) 'Cramming More Components Onto Integrated Circuits', *Electronic Magazine*, 4.
3. *UN Charter*, 26 June 1945, 59 Stat. 1031, 892 UNTS 119.
4. Park, A.T. (2006) 'Incremental Steps for Achieving Space Security: The Need for a New Way of Thinking to Enhance the Legal Regime for Space', *Houston Journal of International Law*, 28(3): 871, 877.
5. See Chayes, A., Handler Chayes, A. and Spitzer, E. (1986) 'Space Weapons: The Legal Context', in Long F.A. *et al.* (eds), *Weapons in Space*. New York: Norton, 193, 196–7.
6. Park, A.T. (2006) 'Incremental Steps for Achieving Space Security: The Need for a New Way of Thinking to Enhance the Legal Regime for Space', *Houston Journal of International Law*, 28(3): 871, 884.
7. *Vienna Convention on the Law of Treaties*, 23 May 1969, UNTS, Vol. 1155, 22 May 1969 and opened for signature on 23 May 1969, entered into force on 27 January 1980.
8. Feinreider, M. (1985) Annual Meeting of the American Society of International Law (New York City).
9. Ibid.
10. See *General and Complete Disarmament*, GA Res 36/97, UN GAOR, 36th sess, 91st plen mtg, UN Doc A/RES/36/97 (1981).
11. Escalera, N.M. (1985) 'Arms Control and US Policy: "Star Wars", Mad, Max and Pershing IIS', *American Society of International Law Proceedings*, 79: 233, 245.
12. *Prevention of an Arms Race in Outer Space*, GA Res 39/59, UN GAOR, 39th sess, 97th plen mtg, UN Doc A/Res/39/59 (1984).
13. Ibid.
14. See e.g. Bridge, R. (1979) 'International Law and Military Activities in Outer Space', *Akron Law Review*, 13: 649, 658.
15. Ramey, R. (2000) 'Armed Conflict on the Final Frontier: The Law of War in Space', *Air Force Law Review*, 48: 1, 157.
16. Conference on Disarmament, Final Record of the 350th Plenary Meeting, UN Doc. CD/PV.350 (1986).

17 See Coyle, P.E. and Rhinelander, J.B. (2002) 'Drawing the Line: the Path to Controlling Weapons in Space', *Disarmament Diplomacy*, 66: 27.
18 'Envoy at UN Opposes Outer Space "Arms Race"' (2000) *BBC Summary of World Broadcasts*, 5 October.
19 Ibid.
20 See Weir, F. (2001) 'Russia Honors First Space Hero', *The Toronto Star*, 12 April, A21.
21 Murray III, W.S. and Antonellis, R. (2003)'China's Space Program: The Dragon Eyes the Moon (and Us)', *Orbis*, 47: 645, 649.
22 Four commercial aircraft were hijacked; two of them were flown into the twin towers of the World Trade Centre in New York City, causing both buildings to collapse. A third aircraft crashed into the Pentagon building in Arlington, Virginia, which houses the headquarters of the US Department of Defence and the US armed forces. The fourth aircraft crashed near Somerset, Pennsylvania.
23 Bush Jr, G.W., 'Commencement Address' (Speech delivered at the US Military Academy at West Point, 1 June 2002). A full text of the speech is reproduced by the *New York Times*, 1 June 2002 and is available at www.nytimes.com/2002/06/01/international/02PTEX-WEB.html (accessed 14 May 2013).
24 Ku, C. (2003) 'When Can Nations Go to War? Politics and Change in the UN Security System', *Michigan Journal of International Law*, 24(4): 1077, 1099.
25 For details on what a Van Allen belt is and its dynamics, see e.g. 'Van Allen Belt', *Encyclopaedia Britannica*, [online] available at www.britannica.com/EBchecked/topic/622563/Van-Allen-radiation-belt (accessed 16 March 2014), noting that the belts are a danger to the sensitive components of satellites at best and agitation that influences the composition by various activities can be disastrous.
26 *UN Charter*, 26 June 1945, 59 Stat. 1031, 892 UNTS 119.
27 See e.g. Lobel, J. and Ratner, M. (1999) 'Bypassing The Security Council: Ambiguous Authorizations to Use Force, Cease-Fires and the Iraqi Inspection Regime', *American Journal of International Law*, 93(1): 124, [online] available at: http://0-au.westlaw.com.library.newcastle.edu.au:80/Find/Default.wl?DB=PROFILER%2DWLD&DocName=0192624101&FindType=h&AP=&mlac=FY&fn=_top&utid=%7b96872FEC-48D9-4663-936C-1639937296E5%7d&rs=WLAU6.06&mt=WestlawAustralia&vr=2.0&sv=Split&sp=UNewcastle-2003 (accessed 13 August 2014).
28 *UN Charter*, 26 June 1945, 59 Stat. 1031, 892 UNTS 119.
29 *Definition of Aggression*, GA Res 3314, UN GAOR, 29th sess, 2319th plen mtg, UN Doc A/RES/3314 (1974).
30 Hurwitz, B.A. (1986) *The Legality of Space Militarization*. Amsterdam: Elsevier Publishers, 174.
31 Ibid., 176 (citing Radio Moscow, 17 August 17 1985 and 2 October 1985).
32 UN General Assembly, 56th General Assembly, First Committee, Disarmament and International Security Committee, 18th Meeting, GA/DIS/3421, 25 October 2010.
33 Ibid.
34 See Primack, J.R. and Abrams, N.E. (2002) 'Invited Talk at Conference on Science and the Search for Meaning: Star Wars Forever? – A Cosmic Perspective', 1, [online] available at http://0-physics.ucsc.edu.library.newcastle.edu.au:80/cosmo/UNESCOr.pdf (accessed 25 September 2013).
35 Ibid.
36 Ibid.
37 Ibid.
38 Ibid.

88 Discarding law by analogy

39 Primack, J.R. and Abrams, N.E. (2002) 'Invited Talk at Conference on Science and the Search for Meaning: Star Wars Forever? – A Cosmic Perspective', 1, [online] available at http://0-physics.ucsc.edu.library.newcastle.edu.au:80/cosmo/UNESCOr.pdf (accessed 25 September 2013).
40 UN General Assembly, 56th General Assembly, First Committee, The Disarmament and International Security Committee, 18th Meeting, GA/DIS/3421, 25 October 2010.
41 Ibid.
42 See e.g. Arms Control Association, (2005) 'Action/Reaction: US Space Weaponization and China', [online] available at www.armscontrol.org (accessed 12 December 2013).
43 Williams, C.D. (1995) 'Space: The Cluttered Frontier', *Journal of Air Law and Commerce*, 60: 1139, 1146.
44 Benkö, M. (2005) 'The Problem of Space Debris: A Valid Case against the Use of Aggressive Military systems in Outer Space?' in Benkö, M. and Scrogl, Kai-Uwe (eds) (2005) *Current Problems and Perspectives for Future Regulation*. Utrecht: Eleven International Publishing, 160.
45 Scheetz, L. (2006) 'Infusing Environmental Ethics into the Space Weapons Dialogue', *Georgetown International Environmental Law Review*, 19: 57, 70.
46 Williams, C.D. (1995) 'Space: The Cluttered Frontier', *Journal of Air Law and Commerce*, 60: 1139, 1145–6.
47 Ibid.
48 Benkö, M. (2005) 'The Problem of Space Debris: A Valid Case against the Use of Aggressive Military systems in Outer Space?' in Benkö, M. and Scrogl, Kai-Uwe (eds) (2005) *Current Problems and Perspectives for Future Regulation*. Utrecht: Eleven International Publishing, 150.
49 Press Release (2004) 'Conference on Disarmament, China and Russia Present New Contributions to Conference on Banning Weapons in Outer Space', [online] available at www.unog.ch/news2/documents/newsen/dc04033e.htm (accessed 5 June 2012).
50 Scheetz, L. (2006) 'Infusing Environmental Ethics into the Space Weapons Dialogue', *Georgetown International Environmental Law Review*, 19: 57, 59.
51 *Treaty on Principles Governing the Activities of States in the Exploration and Use of Outer Space, Including the Moon and Other Celestial Bodies*, opened for signature 27 January 1967, 18 UST 2410, Article VI.
52 Ibid., Article VII.
53 Finch Jr, E.R. (1994) 'Heavenly Junk', *Fletcher Forum of World Affairs*, 18: 129.
54 *Convention on Registration of Objects Launched Into Outer Space*, UN GAOR, 29th Sess., UN Doc. A/15020 (1974) [hereinafter *Registration Convention*] Article II (1).
55 Ibid.
56 Ibid.
57 Ibid., Article VI.
58 See Weiss, E.B. (1989) *In Fairness to Future Generations: International Law, Common Patrimony, and Intergenerational Equity*. New York: Transnational Publishers.
59 See Damrosch, L. (1989) 'Politics across Borders: Nonintervention and Nonforcible Influence of Domestic Affairs', *American Journal of International Law*, 83: 3.
60 *Military and Paramilitary Activities In and Against Nicaragua (Nicaragua v. US)* (Merits) (1986) ICJ Rep 14, 534.
61 Ibid., para 202, Nicaragua (n 23).

62 Joyner, C.C. and Lotrionte, C. (2001) 'Information Warfare as International Coercion: Elements of a Legal Framework', *European Journal of International Law*, 12(5): 825, 848.
63 Buchan, R. (2012) 'Cyber Attacks: Unlawful Uses of Force or Prohibited Interventions?', *Journal of Conflict and Security Law*, 17(2): 211, 221.
64 See Office of General Counsel, US Department of Defence (1999) 'An Assessment of International Legal Issues in Information Operations', 49, [online] available at www.au.af.mil/au/awc/awcgate/dod-io-legal/dod-io-legal.pdf (accessed 14 April 2003).
65 Ibid.
66 Ibid.
67 See Hildreth, S. (2001) 'Congressional Research Service (CRS) Report for Congress', *CYBERWARFARE*, 9, [online] available at www.fas.org.library.newcastle.edu.au/irp/crs/RL30735.pdf (accessed 12 October 2012).
68 Ibid.
69 Ibid.
70 International Telecommunications Union (1982). For details, see UN Doc. A AC.105 213 for a description of the ITU regulations, UN Doc. A AC.105 196, Annex IV (1977).
71 Ibid.
72 See e.g. Barkham, J. (2009) 'Information Warfare and International Law on the Use of Force', *New York University Journal of International Law and Politics*, 34(1): 57.
73 Joyner, C.C. and Lotrionte, C. (2001) 'Information Warfare as International Coercion: Elements of a Legal Framework', *European Journal of International Law*, 12(5): 825, 860.
74 Ibid.
75 *UN Charter*, 26 June 1945, 59 Stat. 1031, 892 UNTS 119.
76 See also Haslam, E. (2000) 'Information Warfare: Technological Changes and International Law', *Journal of Conflict and Security Law*, 5(2): 157.

Conclusion

In the twenty-first century, there is a sustained focus by military powers on technology owing to its centrality in integrating kinetic battle platforms and equally the force multiplier effect in asymmetrical warfare. In this regard, Manabrata Guha notes:

> the future of military strategy [is] centrally premised on information and its integration 'with systems of weaponry and warriors for a seamless sensor-to-shooter flow. Linking these with capabilities of maneuver, strike, logistics and protection' would be critical in exploiting the Observation, Orientation, Decision, Action [OODA] Loop of an adversary.[1]

In the international arena, any threat to global security is a problem shared by all States, particularly when new technology affords the opportunity to develop devastating weaponry in an already over militarised world. Military conflicts continue to grow in number and lethality, with States largely paying only lip-service to the importance of national, regional and international peace and security despite the fact that the collective security established by the UN is specifically geared to de-escalate conflict (in form and substance) in favour of peaceful settlement. While the *UN Charter* does not absolutely prohibit the use of force in all circumstances, it seeks to ensure that use of force is in the common good. As the use of military force becomes more sophisticated and complicated it is imperative that the UN and international community take concrete, defined steps in embedding disarmament principles regarding military activities. Of importance is the need to forestall value added military uses of the digital commons, since various military uses appeal to military powers (major, medium and small) due to low-cost entry barriers creating States' appetites to increase coercive actions.[2]

In certain aspects, the existence of the UN as a quasi-universal international institution *has* fundamentally changed the character of the international system and the post-World War II international security system. Despite a number of (sometimes significant) failings, the *UN Charter* framework has often shown itself capable of adapting to a variety of new tasks. Given the attraction of force multiplication through the meshing of kinetic and non-kinetic phenomena, States are currently reticent to regulate a new means of war whose use offers significant leeway to circumvent the law, yet bolsters asymmetrical war that limits human causalities (civilians and soldiers) and cuts down the high expense of modern conventional weaponry. It is unsettling looking back and reflecting on the present that often 'attempts at pre-emptively limiting military technologies prior to their invention have been largely unsuccessful',[3] yet the most effective avenue is prohibition that preempts new technologies. This has been shown to be effective but unfortunately in only a couple of instances; for example the ban on biological weapons found in the 1925 *Gas Protocol* and the 1972 *Biological Weapons Convention*.[4]

In the context of information warfare activities, the extant regime on the use of force does not as yet concretely address and seek to resolve its ambiguities and complexities, thus offering no real clarification on the emergence of new boundless theatres of conflict.[5] This book concludes with Philip Stevens assertion that:

> A multi-polar world has been predicted, but as always seemed to be perched safely on the horizon. Now it has rushed quite suddenly into the present . . . The transition to a new order is likely to see more rivalry and competition than co-operation. The facts of interdependence cannot be wished away but they will certainly be tested. It is going to be a bumpy ride.[6]

Notes

1 Guha, M. (2013) *Reimagining War in the 21st Century: From Clausewitz to Network-Centric Warfare*. Oxford: Routledge, 93.
2 See e.g. Manabrata Guha, M. (2013) Reimagining War in the 21st Century: From Clausewitz to Network-Centric Warfare. Oxford: Routledge, 113.
3 Richards, P. and Schmitt, M. (1999) 'Mars meets Mother Nature: Protecting the Environment during Armed Conflict', *Stetson Law Review*, 28: 1047, 1083.
4 Ibid.
5 Greenberg, L.T., Goodman, S.E. and Soo Hoo, K.J. (1997) *Information Warfare and International Law*. Institute for National Strategic Studies, National Defense University, Washington, DC, chapter 4.
6 Stephens, P. (2010) 'On the Way to a New Global Balance', *Financial Times*. London, 16 December 2010.

Bibliography

Anderson, R.H. and Feldman, P.M. (1999) *Securing the US Defense Information Infrastructure: A Proposed Approach*. Santa Monica, CA: RAND.

Andrews, D.P. (1996) *Report of the Defense Science Board Task Force on Information Warfare Defense*. Washington, DC: Office of the Secretary of Defense.

Anonymous (2008) 'War, Redefined; Even Before Russian Troops Arrived, Georgian Government Websites Were under Cyber Attack', *Los Angeles Times*, 17 August, Part A, p. 25.

Arms Control Association (2005) 'Action/Reaction: US Space Weaponization and China', [online] available at www.armscontrol.org.

Astronomy Magazine (2008) 'US Successfully Destroys Satellite', 21 February, [online] available at www.astronomy.com/news-observing/news/2008/02/us%20successfully%20destroys%20satellite.

Barkham, J. (2001) 'Information Warfare and International Law on the Use of Force', *New York University Journal of International Law and Politics*, 34(1).

Bartlett, H.C. (1996) 'Force Planning, Military Revolutions and the Tyranny of Technology', *Strategic Review*, 24(4).

Bechhoefer, B. (1973) 'The *Nuclear Test Ban Treaty* in Retrospect', *Case Western Reserve Journal of International Law*, 4(13).

Bekey, I. (1995) 'Force Projection from Space' in Air Force Scientific Advisory Board, *New World Vistas: Air and Space Power for the 21st Century: Space Applications Volume*. Washington, DC: USAF Scientific Advisory Board.

Benkö, M. (2005) 'The Problem of Space Debris: A Valid Case against the Use of Aggressive Military systems in Outer Space?', in Benkö, M. and Scrogl, Kai-Uwe (eds) (2005) *Current Problems and Perspectives for Future Regulation*. Utrecht: Eleven International Publishing.

Blum, Y. (1986) 'The Legality of State Response to Acts of Terrorism', in Netanyahu, B. (ed.) *Terrorism: How the West Can Win*. New York: Farrar, Straus & Giroux.

Bowcott, O. (2013) 'Outer Space Demilitarisation Agreement Threatened By New Technologies', [online] available at www.theguardian.com/science/2013/sep/11/outer-space-demilitarisation-weapons-technologies.

Bowers, D.C. (1998) 'Information Warfare: The Computer Revolution is Altering How Future Wars will be Conducted', *Armed Forces Journal International*, 38–9.

Bridge, R. (1979) 'International Law and Military Activities in Outer Space', *Akron Law Review* (13).

Brownlie, I. (1963) *International Law and the Use of Force by States*. Oxford: Clarendon Press.

Bibliography

Buchan, R. (2012) 'Cyber Attacks: Unlawful Uses of Force or Prohibited Interventions?', *Journal of Conflict and Security Law*, 17(2).
Burnell, Scott (2001) 'US Computer Security Called Inadequate' *United Press International* (27 September), [online] available at www.upi.com/Science_News/2001/09/26/US-computer-security-called-inadequate/UPI-36121001543964/.
Bush Jr, G.W. (2002) 'Commencement Address' (Speech delivered at the US Military Academy at West Point, 1 June).
Cabinet Office (2012) 'The UK Cyber Security Strategy: Report on Progress', December 2012, Forward Plans', 2, [online] available at www.gov.uk/government/uploads/system/uploads/attachment_data/file/265402/Cyber_Security_Strategy_Forward_Plans_3-Dec-12_1.pdf.
Chatham House (2005) 'Principles of International Law on the Use of Force by States in Self-Defence', *Working Paper, ILP WP 05/0*, [online] available at www.chathamhouse.org/publications/papers/view/108106.
Chayes, A., Handler Chayes, A. and Spitzer, E. (1986) 'Space Weapons: The Legal Context', in Long F.A. et al. (eds), *Weapons in Space*. New York: Norton.
Cheng, B. (1983) 'Definitional Issues in Space Law: The "Peaceful Use" of Outer Space, including the Moon and Other Celestial Bodies', *Journal of Space Law*, 11.
Cheng, B. (1997) *Studies in International Space Law*. Oxford: Clarendon Press.
Collins, J.M. (1989) *Military Space Forces: The Next 50 Years*. Washington, DC: Pergamon-Brassey's.
Condron, S. (1999) 'Justification for Unilateral Action in Response to the Iraqi Threat: A Critical Analysis of Operation Desert Fox', *Military Law Review*, 161.
Conference on Disarmament, Final Record of the 350th Plenary Meeting, UN Doc CD/PV.350 (1986).
Convention on International Liability for Damage Caused by Space Objects, opened for signature 29 March 1972, 961 UNTS 187, Article 1(b) (entered into force 1 September 1972).
Convention on Registration of Objects Launched into Outer Space, UN GAOR, 29th Sess., UN Doc. A/15020 (1974) Article II (1).
Coughlin, T. (2011) 'The Future of Robotic Weaponry and the Law of Armed Conflict: Irreconcilable Differences?', *UCL Jurisprudence Review*, 67–8.
Coyle, P.E. and Rhinelander, J.B. (2002) 'Drawing the Line: the Path to Controlling Weapons in Space', *Disarmament Diplomacy*, 66.
Creekman, D.M. (2002) 'A Helpless America? An Examination of the Legal Options Available to the United States in Response to Various Cyber-attacks from China', *American University International Law Review*, 17(3).
Crimes of War Project, Byers, M. (2003) 'Iraq and the "Bush Doctrine" of Pre-emptive Self-Defence', [online] available at www.crimesofwar.org/expert/bush-byers.html.
Crimes of War Project, Koskiennemi, M. (2003) 'Iraq and the "Bush Doctrine" of Pre-emptive Self-Defence', [online] available at www.crimesofwar.org/expert/bush-koskenniemi.html.
Crowley, K. (Cold War Museum) (2008, 20 May) 'The Strategic Defense Initiative (SDI): Star Wars', [online] available at www.coldwar.org/articles/80s/sdi-starwars.asp.
Dahinden, E. (2005) 'The Future of Arms Control Law: Towards a New Regulatory Approach and New Regulatory Techniques', *Journal of Conflict and Security Law* 263, 269.

Bibliography 95

Damrosch, L. (1989) 'Politics Across Borders: Non-intervention and No Forcible Influence of Domestic Affairs', *American Journal of International Law*, 83.

David, L. (2003) 'Pentagon Report: China's Space Warfare Tactics Aimed at US Supremacy', *Space*, 1 August, [online] available at www.space.com/news/china_dod_030801.html.

Declaration Concerning Friendly Relations, GA Res 2625, UN GAOR, 25th sess, 1883rd plen mtg, UN Doc A/RES/2625 (1970).

Definition of Aggression, G.A. Res. 3314, Annex, art. 2, UN GAOR, 29th Sess., UN Doc. A/RES/3314/Annex (14 December 1974).

Dembling, P.G. and Arons, D.M. (1967) 'The Evolution of the *Outer Space Treaty*', *Journal of Air Law and Commerce*, 33: 419.

Denning, D.E. (1999) *Information Warfare and Security*. Essex: Addison-Wesley Longman.

Department of Information Technology (2011) 'Ministry of Communications and Information Technology, Government of India: Discussion Draft on National Cyber Security', 5, [online] available at http://deity.gov.in/content/discussion-draft-national-cyber-security-policy.

Dinstein, Y. (1994) *War, Aggression, and Self-Defence* (2nd edn). Cambridge: Cambridge University Press.

Editorial (1992) 'Military Eyes CRAF-like System for Commercial Satellites', *Aerospace News*, 21 February, 285.

Editorial (2001) 'Pentagon Web Sites Blocked; Threat of "Code Red" Computer "Worm" Prompts Safeguards', *Washington Post*, 24 July, A5.

Elagab, O.Y. (1992) 'Economic Measures against Developing Countries', *International and Comparative Law Quarterly*, 41(3).

'Envoy at UN Opposes Outer Space "Arms Race"' (2000) *BBC Summary of World Broadcasts*, 5 October.

Escalera, N.M. (1985) 'Arms Control and US Policy: "Star Wars", Mad, Max and Pershing IIS', *American Society of International Law Proceedings*, 79.

Executive Office of the President (2011) 'International Strategy for Cyberspace: Prosperity, Security, and Openness in a Networked World', [online] available at www.whitehouse.gov/sites/default/files/rss_viewer/international_strategy_for_cyberspace.pdf.

Fawcett, J.E.S. (1984) *Outer Space: New Challenges to Law and Policy*. Oxford: Clarendon Press.

Feaver, P. (1998) 'Blowback: Information Warfare and the Dynamics of Coercion', *Security Studies*, 7.

Feinreider, M. (1985) Annual Meeting of the American Society of International Law (New York City).

Fidler, S., Sevastopulo, D. and Ward, A. (2007) 'US Concedes Danger of Cyber-attack', *Financial Times Online*. 7 September, [online] available at http://0-search.ft.com.library.newcastle.edu.au/ftArticle?queryText=People%27s+Liberation+Army%2C+computer&aje=false&_id=070905010503&ct=0

Finch Jr, E.R. (1994) 'Heavenly Junk', *Fletcher Forum of World Affairs*, 18.

Friesen, T.L. (2009) 'Resolving Tomorrow's Conflicts Today: How New Developments within the UN Security Council can be Used to Combat Cyberwarfare', *Naval Law Review*, 58.

Gallagher, M. (1986) 'Legal Aspects of the Strategic Defense Initiative', *Military Law Review*, 111.

Garamone, J. (2010) 'Alexander Details US Cyber Command Gains', *American Forces Press Service*, 24 September, [online] available at www.defense.gov/news/newsarticle.aspx?id=61014.

General and Complete Disarmament, GA Res 36/97, UN GAOR, 36th sess, 91st plen mtg, UN Doc A/RES/36/97 (1981).

Goedhuis, D. (1981) 'Some Recent Trends in the Interpretation and the Implementation of the Rules of International Space Law', *Columbia Journal of Transnational Law*, 19.

Gompert, D.C. and Lachow, I. (2000) 'Transforming US Forces: Lessons from a Wider Revolution', *Rand Issue Paper*, [online] available at www.rand.org/publications/IP/IP193/.

Gorove, S. (1973) 'Arms Control Provisions in the *Outer Space Treaty*: A Scrutinizing Reappraisal', *Georgia Journal of International and Comparative Law*, 3.

Greenberg, L.T., Goodman, S.E. and Soo Hoo, K.J. (1997) *Information Warfare and International Law*. Washington, DC: Institute for National Strategic Studies, National Defense University.

Guha, M. (2013) *Reimagining War in the 21st Century: From Clausewitz to Network-Centric Warfare*. Oxford: Routledge.

Halpern, J. (1985) 'Antisatellite Weaponry: The High Road to Destruction', *Boston University International Law Journal*, 3.

Haslam, E. (2000) 'Information Warfare: Technological Changes and International Law', *Journal of Conflict and Security Law*, 5(2): 157.

Henkin, L. (1979) *How Nations Behave* (2nd edn). New York: Columbia University Press.

Hildreth, S. (2001) 'Congressional Research Service (CRS) Report for Congress', *Cyberwarfare*, [online] available at http://fas.org/irp/crs/RL30735.pdf.

Hosenball, M. (2007) 'Whacking Hackers', *Newsweek*, 15 October, 10.

Hunker, J., Hutchinson, B. and Margulies, J. (2008) 'Role and Challenges for Sufficient Cyber-Attack Attribution', *Institute for Information Infrastructure Protection, White Paper*, [online] available at www.thei3p.org.library.newcastle.edu.au/docs/publications/whitepaper-attribution.pdf.

Hurwitz, B.A. (1986) *The Legality of Space Militarization*. Amsterdam: Elsevier Publishers, 174.

Hurwitz, B. (1994) 'Non-Proliferation and Free Access to Outer Space: The Dual-Use Dilemma of the *Outer Space Treaty* and the Missile Technology Control Regime', *High Technology Law Journal*, 9.

Jasani, B. (1987) 'Space Weapons and International Security – An Overview' in Jasani, B. (ed.) *Space Weapons and International Security*. Oxford: Oxford University Press.

John J. Meyer III, J.J. (1993) 'JTF Communications: The Way Ahead'. *Military Law Review*, 85.

Joint Chiefs of Staff (1998) *Department of Defence Joint Doctrine for Information Operations (I-9 Joint Publication 3-13)*. Washington, DC: US Department of Defence.

Joint Chiefs of Staff (2001) *Department of Defence Dictionary of Military and Associated Terms (Joint Publication 1-02)*. Washington, DC: US Department of Defence.

Joyner, C.C. and Lotrionte, C. (2001) 'Information Warfare as International Coercion: Elements of a Legal Framework', *European Journal of International Law*, 12(5).

Kanuck, S.P. (1996) 'Recent Development, Information Warfare: New Challenges for Public International Law', *Harvard International Law Journal*, 37(1).
Kiernan, V. (1991) 'War Tests Satellites' Prowess, Military Space Systems Put to Work during Desert Storm Conflict', *Space News*, 21 January.
Killette, K. (1991) 'Iraq Net Critical Target', *Communications Week*, 21 January, 60.
Ku, C. (2003) 'When Can Nations Go to War? Politics and Change in the UN Security System', *Michigan Journal of International Law*, 24(4).
Kunich, J. (1997) 'Planetary Defense: The Legality of Global Survival', *Air Force Law Review*, 41.
Landler, M. and Markoff, J. 'After Computer Siege on Estonia, War Fears Turn to Cyberspace', *New York Times*, 29 May, A1.
Legality of the Threat or Use of Nuclear Weapons (Advisory Opinion) (1996) ICJ Rep 226, 105.
Lewis, J.A. (2013) 'On the Offensive in the Cyberspace Arms Race', *The Washington Post*, 13 October, [online] available at www.japantimes.co.jp/news/2013/10/13/business/on-the-offensive-in-the-cyber space-arms-race/#.U05G3WDjiM8.
Liability Convention, opened for signature 29 March 1972, 961 UNTS 187, Article 3 (entered into force 1 September 1972).
Libicki, M. and Duncan, N. (1998) 'A Primer on the Employment of Non-Lethal Weapons', *Naval Law Review*, 45.
Limited Test Ban Treaty, opened for signature 5 August 1963, 480 UNTS 43 (entered into force 10 October 1963).
Lobel, J. and Ratner, M. (1999) 'Bypassing the Security Council: Ambiguous Authorizations to Use Force, Cease-Fires and the Iraqi Inspection Regime', *American Journal of International Law*, 93(1), [online] available at http://0-au.westlaw.com.library.newcastle.edu.au:80/Find/Default.wl?DB=PROFILER%2DWLD&DocName=0108060701&FindType=h&AP=&mlac=FY&fn=_top&utid=%7b96872FEC-48D9-4663-936C-1639937296E5%7d&rs=WLAU6.06&mt=WestlawAustralia&vr=2.0&sv=Split&sp=UNewcastle-2003.
Lynn, W. (2011) 'Announcement of the Department of Defense Cyberspace Strategy at the National Defense University', [online] available at www.pentagonchannel.mil/onestory_popup.aspx?pid=FttPuXny5i7D8p1hC0rgnXrveieDVeMW.
Madsen, W. (1993) 'Intelligence Agency Threats to Computer Security', *International Journal of Intelligence and Counter Intelligence*, 6.
Markoff, J. (2008a) 'Before the Gunfire, Cyberattacks', *New York Times*, 13 August, A1, [online] available at www.nytimes.com/2008/08/13/technology/13cyber.html.
Markoff, J. (2008b) 'Georgia Takes a Beating in the Cyberwar with Russia', *New York Times Online*, 11 August, [online] available at http://bits.blogs.nytimes.com/2008/08/11/georgia-takes-a-beating-in-the-cyberwar-with-russia/?scp=1&sq=cyberwarfare&st=cse.
Markoff, M. (1976) 'Disarmament and "Peaceful Purposes" Provisions in the 1967 Outer Space Treaty', *Journal of Space Law*, 3(1).
Matte, N. (1987) 'A Treaty for "Star Peace"', in Matte, N. (ed.) *Arms Control and Disarmament in Outer Space: Lecture-Seminars Given at the Centre for Research of Air and Space Law* (Vol. 2). Montreal: Centre for Research of Air and Space Law, 190.
Meyer, J.J. (1993) 'JTF Communications: The Way Ahead', *Military Law Review*, 43(3).

Military and Paramilitary Activities In and Against Nicaragua (Nicaragua v. US), 1986 ICJ (June 27).

Minnick, W. (2011) 'China's PLA Involved in Cyber Espionage: Report', [online] available at www.defensenews.com/article/20111110/DEFSECT04/111100310/China-s-PLA-Involved-Cyber-Espionage-Report.

Moore, G.E. (1965) 'Cramming more Components Onto Integrated Circuits', *Electronic Magazine*, 4.

Moore, J.B. (1906) *A Digest of International Law as Embodied in Diplomatic Discussions, Treaties and other International Agreements, International Awards, the Decisions of Municipal Courts, and the Writings of Jurists* (Vol. 2). Washington, DC: US Government Print Office.

Moore, M.S. (2010) 'War With Iran? Stuxnet May Be First Cybersalvo', *Christian Science Monitor*, 28 September, [online] available at www.psmag.com/navigation/politics-and-law/war-with-iran-stuxnet-may-be-first-cybersalvo-23321/.

Morenoff, J. (1973) *World Peace Through Space Law*. Charlottesville, VA: Michie Company.

Morgan, R. (1994) 'Military Use of Commercial Communication Satellites: A New Look at the *Outer Space Treaty* and "Peaceful Purposes"', *Journal of Air Law and Commerce*, 60.

Mosteshar, S. (2004) 'Militarization of Outer Space: Legality and Implications for the Future of Space Law', *Proceedings of the Colloquium on the Law of Outer Space*, 47.

Mueller, P. and Yadegari, B. (2013) 'The Stuxnet Worm', [online] available at www.cs.arizona.edu/~collberg/Teaching/466-566/2012/Resources/presentations/2012/topic9-final/report.pdf.

Murray III, W.S. and Antonellis, R. (2003) 'China's Space Program: The Dragon Eyes the Moon (and Us)', *Orbis*, 47.

NATO (2010) 'Strategic Concept for the Defence and Security of the Members of the North Atlantic Treaty Organization', [online] 19, available at www.nato.int/lisbon2010/strategic-concept-2010-eng.pdf.

NATO (2011) 'Working with the Private Sector to Deter Cyber Attacks', [online] available at www.nato.int/cps/en/natolive/news_80764.htm.

News24.com (2003) 'China Looking at "Space Force"', [online] available at www.news24.com/News24/Technology/News/0,,2-13-1443_1433115,00.html.

O'Donnell, B.T. and Kraska, J.C. (2002) 'Humanitarian Law: Developing International Rules for the Digital Battlefield', *Journal of Conflict and Security Law*, 8(1).

Office of General Counsel, US Department of Defence (1999) 'An Assessment of International Legal Issues in Information Operations', 49 [online] available at www.au.af.mil/ au/awc/awcgate/dod-io-legal/dod-io-legal.pdf.

Outer Space Treaty, opened for signature 27 January 1967, 610 UNTS 205 (entered into force 10 October 1967).

Owens, W.A. (1995–96) 'The American Revolution in Military Affairs', *Joint Force Quarterly*, 37.

Park, A.T. (2006) 'Incremental Steps for Achieving Space Security: The Need for a New Way of Thinking to Enhance the Legal Regime for Space', *Houston Journal of International Law*, 28(3).

Perry, J.D. (2000) 'Operation Allied Force: The View from Beijing', *Aerospace Power Journal* 14(2).

Petersen, J.H. (1993) 'Info Wars', *Naval Institute Proceedings*, 119(5) (May).

Press Release (2004) 'Conference on Disarmament, China and Russia Present New Contributions to Conference on Banning Weapons in Outer Space', [online] available at www.unog.ch/news2/documents/newsen/dc04033e.htm.

Prevention of an Arms Race in Outer Space, GA Res 39/59, UN GAOR, 39th sess, 97th plen mtg, UN Doc A/Res/39/59 (1984).

Primack, J.R. and Abrams, N.E. (2002) 'Invited Talk at Conference on Science and the Search for Meaning: Star Wars Forever? – A Cosmic Perspective', 1 [online] available at http://0-physics.ucsc.edu.library.newcastle.edu.au:80/cosmo/UNESCOr.pdf.

Ramey, R. (2000) 'Armed Conflict on the Final Frontier: The Law of War in Space', *Air Force Law Review*, 48.

Reijnen, G.C.M. (1982) 'The Term "Peaceful" in Space Law', *Proceedings of the 25th Colloquium on the Law of Outer Space*. Paris: International Law Association.

Report of the Commission to Assess United States National Security Space Management and Organization (2001) [online] available at www.defenselink.mil/pubs/space20010111.html.

'Report of Secretary of State Rogers' (1972) *Department of State Bulletin*, 67.

Richards, P. and Schmitt, M. (1999) 'Mars meets Mother Nature: Protecting the Environment during Armed Conflict', *Stetson Law Review*, 28.

Ricks, T. (2001) 'Space is Playing Field for Newest War Game: Air Force Exercise Shows Shift in Focus', *Washington Post*, 29 January.

Romero, P.M. (2006) 'An Immunological Approach to Counter-Terrorism and Infrastructure Defense Law in Electronic Domains', *International Journal of Law and Information Technology*, 101, 104.

Russell, R. (1958) *A History of the UN Charter: The Role of the United States, 1940–1945*. Washington, DC: Brookings Institution.

Schachter, O. (1984) 'International Law: The Right of States to Use Armed Force', *Michigan Law Review*, 82.

Scheetz, L. (2006) 'Infusing Environmental Ethics into the Space Weapons Dialogue', *Georgetown International Environmental Law Review*, 19.

Schmitt, M. (1999) 'Computer Network Attack and the Use of Force in International Law: Thoughts on a Normative Framework', *Columbia Journal of Transnational Law*, 37.

Schmitt, M.N. (ed.) (2013) *Tallinn Manual on the International Law Applicable to Cyber Warfare*. Cambridge: Cambridge University Press, 45.

Schwelb, E. (1964) 'The *Nuclear Test Ban Treaty* and International Law', *American Journal of International Law*, 58.

Serabian, J.A. (2000) 'Information Operations Issue Manager, Central Intelligence Agency before the Joint Economic Committee on Cyber Threats and the US Economy', [online] available at www.odci.gov/cia/publicaffairs/speeches/cyberthreats022300.html.

Shaw, M. (2014) 'Principles of International Law on the Use of Force by States in Self-Defence', *Working Paper, ILP WP 05/0*, 17–18, [online] available at www.chathamhouse.org/publications/papers/view/108106.

Simma, B. (ed.) (1994) *The Charter of the United Nations: A Commentary*. Oxford: Oxford University Press.

Simpson, G. (2014) 'Principles of International Law on the Use of Force by States in Self-Defence', *Working Paper, ILP WP 05/0*, 18, [online] available at www.chathamhouse.org/publications/papers/view/10810.

100 Bibliography

Sklerov, M.J. (2009) 'Solving the Dilemma of State Responses to Cyberattacks: A Justification for the Use of Active Defenses Against States Who Neglect Their Duty to Prevent', *Military Law Review*, 201.

Sourbès, I. and Boyer, Y. (1999) 'Technical Aspects of Peaceful and Non-Peaceful Uses of Space' in Jasani, B. (ed.) *Peaceful and Non-Peaceful Uses of Space: Problems of Definition for the Prevention of an Arms Race*. New York: Taylor & Francis.

Stares, P. (1985) *The Militarization of Space: US Policy, 1945–1984*. Ithaca, NY: Cornell University Press.

Statement of US Ambassador Goldberg, UN GAOR, COPUOS, Legal Subcomm, 5th sess, 62nd mtg, UN Doc A/AC.105/C.2/SR.62 (1966), reprinted in Jasentuliyana, N. (ed.) (1989) *Manual of Space Law* (Vol. 3). New York: Oceana Publications.

Stephens, P. (2010) 'On the Way to a New Global Balance', *Financial Times*. London, 16 December 2010.

Stone, J. (1958) *Aggression and World Order: A Critique of United Nations Theories of Aggression*. Sydney: Maitland.

The Report of the President's Commission on Critical Infrastructure Protection (1997) *Critical Foundations: Protecting America's Infrastructure*, [online] available at www.ciao.gov/PCCIP/PCCIP_Report.pdf.

The White House (2002) *The National Security of the United States of America*, [online] available at www.whitehouse.gov/nsc/nss.html.

Treaty on Principles Governing the Activities of States in the Exploration and Use of Outer Space, Including the Moon and Other Celestial Bodies, opened for signature 27 January 1967, 18 UST 2410.

Treaty on the Limitation of Anti-Ballistic Missile Systems, US–USSR, 26 May 1972, 23 UST 3435.

Tsagourias, N. (2012) 'Cyber Attacks, Self-Defence and the Problem of Attribution', *Journal of Conflict and Security Law*, 17(2).

US Space Command (1998) *Long Range Plan: Implementing USSPACECOM Vision for 2020*. Peterson Air Force Base, Colorado Springs, CO: US Space Command, 21.

US Space Command (2001) 'US Air Force Space Command: Command News', [online] available at www.spacecom.af.mil/hqafspc/news/default.htm.

UN Charter, 26 June 1945, 59 Stat. 1031, 892 UNTS 119.

UN General Assembly, 56th General Assembly, First Committee, The Disarmament and International Security Committee, 18th Meeting, GA/DIS/3421, 25 October 2010.

USAF Scientific Advisory Board (1995) *New World Vistas: Air and Space Power for the 21st Century Report*. Washington, DC: US Department of Defence.

US Air Force (2004) 'Counterspace Operations', *Air Force Doctrine Document 2–2.1*, [online] available at www.fas.org/irp/doddir/usaf/afdd2_2-1.pdf.

US Air Force Cyber Command (n.d.) *Cyberspace 101, Understanding the Cyberspace Domain*, [online] available at www.afcyber.af.mil/library/factsheets/factsheet.asp?id=10784.

US Department of Defence (1999) 'Directive Number 3100.10' § 4.2.1', [online] available at www.dtic.mil/whs/directives/corres/pdf/310010p.pdf.

US Department of Defence (2006) *US Quadrennial Defense Review Report*, Washington, DC: Department of Defence, 58, [online] available at www.defense.gov/home/features/2014/0314_sdr/qdr.aspx.

'Van Allen Belt', *Encyclopaedia Britannica*, [online] available at www.britannica.com/EBchecked/topic/622563/Van-Allen-radiation-belt.

Vienna Convention on the Law of Treaties, 23 May 1969, UNTS, Vol. 1155, 22 May 1969 and opened for signature on 23 May 1969 (entered into force on 27 January 1980).

Vlasic, I. (1991) 'The Legal Aspects of Peaceful and Non-Peaceful Uses of Outer Space' in Jasani, B. (ed.) *Peaceful and Non-Peaceful Uses of Space: Problems of Definition for the Prevention of an Arms Race.* New York: Taylor & Francis.

Waxman, M.C. (2011) 'Cyber Attacks and the Use of Force: Back to the Future of Article 2(4)', *Yale Journal of International Law*, 36(2).

Weir, F. (2001) 'Russia Honors First Space Hero', *The Toronto Star*, 12 April, A21.

Weiss, E.B. (1989) *In Fairness to Future Generations: International Law, Common Patrimony, and Intergenerational Equity.* New York: Transnational Publishers.

Williams, C.D. (1995) 'Space: The Cluttered Frontier', *Journal of Air Law and Commerce*, 60.

Wilske, S. and Schiller, T. (1997) 'International Jurisdiction in Cyberspace: Which States May Regulate the Internet', *Federal Communications Law Journal*, 50.

Wilson, C. (2003) 'Information Operations, Electronic Warfare, and Cyberwar: Capabilities and Related Policy', *Issues 5 Congressional Research Services (CRS) Report for Congress Order Code RL31787*, [online] available at www.fas.org.library.newcastle.edu.au/sgp/crs/natsec/RL31787.pdf.

Wingfield, T. (2000) *The Law of Information Conflict, National Security Law in Cyberspace.* Huntsville, AL: Aegis Research Corporation, 21.

Wong, N.C. (2001) '"Code Red" Creeping Worldwide', *Washington Post*, 2 August.

Zedalis, R. and Wade, C. (1978) 'Anti-Satellite Weapons and the *Outer Space Treaty* of 1967', *California Western International Law Journal*, 8: 461.

Index

Page references to Notes will be followed by the letter 'n'

ABM Treaty see Anti-Ballistic Missile (ABM) Treaty (1972)
ABMs *see* Anti-Ballistic Missiles
Abrams, N.E. 87n, 88n
Agreement on the Prevention of Dangerous Military Activities (1989) 84
Anderson, Robert 3, 8n
Andrews, D.P. 7n, 8n
Anti-Ballistic Missile (ABM) Treaty (1972) 41–3, 51n, 52n; and MAD doctrine 42; 'rightful intent' 42; US withdrawal (2001) 43
Anti-Ballistic Missiles (ABMs) 41, 42
anticipatory State actions, and self-defence 12, 14, 67
Anti-Satellite Weapons (ASATs) 14, 33, 44; intersection of *UN Charter* regime on force and outer space law 34, 37, 42
ARAMCO (Saudi Arabian National Oil Company) 60
armed attack: actual, and right of self-defence 12; concept 10–11, 13, 15, 18–19n; and cyber conflict 57–9; *de minimis* approach to 67
arms control, coercive 59, 78–9
arms race 25
Arons, D.M. 48n
ASATs *see* Anti-Satellite Weapons

Babak Yadegari, B. 68n
'barbed wire' analogy 81

Barkham, Jason 55, 61, 63, 68n, 89n
Bechhoefer, B. 50n
Bekey, I. 52n
Benkö, Marietta 80–1, 88n
Biological Weapons Convention (1972) 92
blockade, armed attack 18n
Blum, Y. 19n
bombardment, armed attack 18n
Bowcott, O. 52n
Boyer, Y. 49n
Brazil 59
breach of stationing agreements, armed attack 18–19n
Bridge, R. 86n
Brownlie, Ian 19n, 65
Buchan, Russell 83, 89n
Burnell, Scott 7n
Bush, George W., West Point speech (2002) 76–7, 87n
Byers, Michael 13, 20n

Caroline Incident (1837) 12–13
cascade effect, space debris 81
celestial bodies 32, 33, 36, 37
Centre for the Protection of National Infrastructures (CPNI) 3
Charter of the United Nations (UN Charter): acts of war within 14; basic tenets 31; black-letter law 12; challenging 13–14; and cyberwarfare 55, 64, 65, 69n; drafting 9, 12, 13, 76; electronic blockades 62–3; exceptions to

restrictions on use of force 19n; generalities 14–17; Information Warfare 59; intersection on force and outer space law 32–43; and *Outer Space Treaty* (1967) 35; re-orienting peace and security framework 78; self-defence, right of States to respond in 9, 10–13, 35, 64, 85; and use of force 4, 5–6, 9, 11–17, 19n, 32–43, 55, 65, 66, 67, 91
Chayes, A. 86n
Cheng, Bin 37, 38, 47n, 49n
China: ASAT testing (2007) 45; hacking of US DoD computers 2, 26; 'Space Club,' joining of 76; space force strength concept 15
civilian marine and air fleets, armed attack 18n
CNA *see* Computer Network Attack
CNE *see* Computer Network Exploitation
CNI *see* Critical National Infrastructure
code analysis 53
'Code Red' (computer worm) 26
coercive arms control 59, 78–9
Cold War paradigm 4–5, 41, 43
Collins, J.M. 48n
command and control warfare 56
Committee on the Peaceful Uses of Outer Space (COPUOS) 73, 80
Computer Network Attack (CNA) 2, 56
Computer Network Exploitation (CNE) 26
Congressional Research Service (CRS) Report, US (2001) 2
*Convention on International Liability for Damage Caused by Space Object*s *see* Liability Convention (1972)
Convention on Registration of Objects Launched into Outer Space (*Registration Convention*), 1974 82
COPUOS *see* Committee on the Peaceful Uses of Outer Space
corpus juris spatialis 40
Coughlin, Timothy 5, 8n
counterforce 14

counter-restrictionist approach, self-defence rights 11, 12–13
counter-space capabilities/operations 25, 43
Coyle, P.E. 87n
CPNI *see* Centre for the Protection of National Infrastructures
Crimes of War Project 20n
Critical National Infrastructure (CNI) 1, 4, 6, 23; cyberwarfare 53, 60, 65, 66
cross-border shooting, armed attack 18n
Crowley, K. 49n
Cuban Missile Crisis (1962) 77
customary law 12
cyber attacks 26, 59, 85; classifications and analytical models 55–7
Cyber Command, US 16, 53, 68n
Cyber Security Strategy Report, UK 3
cyber space 6, 83–7; whether conclusive multilateral framework 83–4; as fifth domain 4, 25–7; legal consequences of events/activities 3; legal thresholds for information warfare, rethinking 85; non-intervention principle, refocus on 83; and use of force 14, 15
cyber surveillance 26
cyberwarfare 53–70; Critical National Infrastructure (CNI) 53, 60, 65, 66; cyber attacks, classifications and analytical models 55–7; cyber conflict along armed attack spectrum 57–9; cyber interpretations and disruptions 56–7; cybersnooping 61–2; whether data property 62; effects-based approach 57; electronic blockades 62–4; geographic component 57; Georgia, attacks on digital ecosystem 2; hacking of US DoD computers by China 2, 26; Information Warfare 59–64, 85; instrument-based approach 57; international law 58, 63, 64, 67; logical component 57; multilateralism 83–4; *Nicaragua Case* (1986) 65, 66, 67, 69n; parameters, non-conventional

attacks 56–7; physical destruction (kinetic force) 59, 60–2; physical network component 57; quantitative evaluation 64–5; risk 2; small- or large-scale attacks 64–5; smokeless warfare 58–9; specific targeting of military facilities 65–6; strict liability approach 57; *Tallin Manual* (*Tallin Manual on International Law Applicable to Cyber Warfare*) 58, 59, 62, 64–5, 66; and *UN Charter* 55, 64, 65, 69n; and use of force 59–65

Dahinden, Erwin 55, 68n
Damrosch, L. 88n
data, whether property 62
David, L. 29n
DDoS *see* Distributed Denial of Service
debris, space 80
Declaration of Friendly Relations (General Assembly, 1970) 10, 18n
Dembling, P.G. 48n
Denning, D.E. 68n
Department of Defense (DoD), US 2, 16, 24, 27, 57, 84
digital commons 3, 6, 9, 15, 16, 28, 72, 91; global 4, 6, 17
disarmament: and *Limited Test Ban Treaty* 39; UN Committee 74, 75; UN Conference on Disarmament (1986) 45, 52n, 75, 86n; UN Conference on Disarmament (2008) 79
Distributed Denial of Service (DDoS) 65
DoD *see* Department of Defense, US
Draft Treaty on the Stationing of Weapons of any Kind in Outer Space 74
Duncan, Nigel 56, 68n

E-Bomb *see* Electromagnetic Pulse Bombs
economic damage 9
economic information warfare 56
economic rights, law of 15
ecosystems, digital 5

effects-based approach, cyberwarfare 57
electromagnetic dominance 26
Electromagnetic Pulse Bombs (E-Bombs) 58
Electromagnetic Pulse (EMP) 34, 39, 45, 50n
electronic blockades 62–4
electronic warfare 26, 56
EMP *see* Electromagnetic Pulse
Escalera, N.M. 86n
Estonia, cyber assault on digital infrastructure (2007) 2, 26, 53, 54, 63

Fawcett, J.E.S. 49n
Feinreider, Martin 73, 86n
Feldman, P.M. 3
fifth domain *see* cyberspace
Finch, Edward 82, 88n
force, use of 9–21; 'all necessary means,' right to use 15, 16; colliding or colluding with cyberwarfare regime 59–64; concept of armed attack 10–11, 13, 15, 18–19n; counter-restrictionist approach 12–13; direct military force in outer space 33–4; exceptions to restrictions on 19n; indirect military force in outer space 33, 34; international law 15, 17; intersection on force and outer space law 32–43; kinetic (physical destruction) *see* physical destruction (kinetic force); non-kinetic *see* non-kinetic force (electronic intrusions); participation by military organized unofficial groups 19n; political independence 10; prohibition in international relations 10; restrictionist approach 11, 12; self-defence, right of States to respond in 9, 10–13, 35, 64, 85; territorial integrity 10, 18n, 59; *UN Charter* 4, 5–6, 9, 11–17, 32–43, 55, 65, 91; unilateral acts, whether permissible 9, 11
fourth domain *see* outer space
Friesen, Toby 27, 29n, 30n, 68n

106   *Index*

Gallagher, M. 49n
Garamone, J. 68n
Gas Protocol (1925) 92
General Assembly, UN 73, 78, 84, 88n; 39th Session (1984) 74; *Declaration of Friendly Relations* (1970) 10, 18n; *Definition of Aggression* Resolution 3314 (1974) 11, 18n; Resolution 1148 (1957) 36; *see also* United Nations
GEO *see* geo-synchronous orbit
Georgia, attacks on digital ecosystem (2008) 2, 26, 53, 54, 63
geo-synchronous orbit (GEO) 25, 43, 79, 80
GIG *see* Global Information Grid
global commons 3, 15, 46, 72; digital 4, 6
Global Information Grid (GIG) 28
global interdependence 3
Global Positioning System (GPS) 8n, 25, 44, 47n
Goedhuis, D. 47n
Gompert, D.C. 7n
Goodman, S.E. 92n
Gorove, S. 50n
GPS *see* Global Positioning System
Greenberg, L.T. 92n
ground-based systems, and space assets 8n
Guha, Manabrata 91, 92n
Gulf War ('Operation Desert Storm,') 1991 1, 33; as first so called 'space war' 43–4

hacker warfare 2, 26, 56
Halpern, J. 48–9n
Handler Chayes, A. 86n
hardware, military 2, 55
Haslam, Emily 68n, 86, 89n
Henkin, Louis 67
High Seas regime 4
High-powered Microwaves (HPM) 58
Hildreth, S. 7n, 89n
Hosenball, M. 7n
HPM *see* High-powered Microwaves
Hunker, J. 21n
Hurewitz, B. 38, 48n, 49n, 51n, 87n

Hutchinson, B. 21n
hypervelocity weapons 33–4, 81; *see also* kinetic weapons; physical destruction (kinetic force)

ICBMs *see* Inter-Continental Ballistic Missiles
ICJ *see* International Court of Justice
India 2
industrial espionage 62
information infrastructures 2, 3–4, 16, 27
information networks 3, 5, 15
information RMA 2, 4, 6, 17, 71
information systems 25
Information Warfare (IW) 4, 16, 27, 56; colliding or colluding with use of force regime 59–64; legal thresholds, rethinking 85
infrastructures: Centre for the Protection of National Infrastructures (CPNI) 3; convergence of civilian and military network nodes 27; Critical National Infrastructure (CNI) 1, 4, 6, 23, 60, 65, 66; information 2, 3–4, 16, 27
instrument-based approach, cyberwarfare 57
integrated battleground platforms 25
intelligence based warfare 56
Inter-Continental Ballistic Missiles (ICBMs) 38, 41, 42
International Court of Justice (ICJ) 83
International Environmental Law Platform 79–82
international law 71, 72, 73, 85; customary rules 83; cyberwarfare 58, 63, 64, 67; outer space 32, 35, 37, 38, 46, 50n, 73; and use of force 15, 17; *see also* cyberwarfare; force, use of; outer space; *Tallin Manual* (*Tallin Manual on International Law Applicable to Cyber Warfare*)
International Strategy for Cyberspace (US) 15
International Telecommunications Convention (ITC) 84
Internet 2, 55; maturation 1, 4

invasion, armed attack 18n
Iran, Stuxnet worm, effect on nuclear program (2009–10) 53–4
Israel 54
ITC see International Telecommunications Convention
IW see Information Warfare

Jasani, B. 47n, 48n
Jennings, Robert 83
Joyner, Christopher C. 20n, 64, 69n, 83, 85, 89n
jus ad bellum (right to war) 5, 10, 35, 67
jus in bello (laws on conduct of war) 5, 35

Kanuk, Sean 71, 86n
Kennedy, John 77
Kennedy, Laura 80
Kiernan, V. 7n, 48n
Killette, K. 48n
kinetic force see physical destruction (kinetic force)
kinetic weapons 1, 6, 14, 33, 81; see also physical destruction (kinetic force)
Korean Peninsula 60
Koskenniemi, Martti 13, 20n
Kraska, James C. 21n, 27, 30n
Ku, C. 87n
Kunich, John 39, 40, 50n

Lachow, I. 7n
land, sea or air forces, armed attack 18n
Langner, Ralph 53
law, discarding by analogy 71–89; 'peaceful purposes' conundrum, resolving 72–6
Law of Armed Conflict 17
LEO see low-Earth orbit
Liability Convention (1972) 40–1, 50n, 51n
Libicki, Martin 56, 68n
Limited Test Ban Treaty (1963) 38–40, 47n, 49n, 50n; object and purposes 38, 39
Lobel, J. 87n

Lotrionte, Catherine 20n, 69n, 83, 85, 89n
low-Earth orbit (LEO) 25, 79, 80
Lynn, W. 20n

MAD doctrine see Mutual Assured Destruction doctrine
Madsen, W. 20n
malware (malicious software) 53, 58
Margulies, J. 21n
Markoff, J. 29n, 30n
Markoff, M. 48n
Maser see Microwave Amplification by Stimulated Emission of Radiation
Matte, Nicholas 47–8n
Meyer, John J. 48n
Microwave Amplification by Stimulated Emission of Radiation (Maser) 58
'microwave' technology 33
militarisation of outer space 4, 9, 33, 43–5, 47n, 74–5
military facilities, specific targeting of 65–6
Ministry of Defence (MoD), UK 27
Minnick, W. 29n
MoD see Ministry of Defence, UK
moon 32, 37
Moore, G.E. 86n; 'Moore's Law' 71
Moore, J. 19n
Moore, M.S. 68n
Morenoff, J. 49n
Morgan, R. 47n, 52n
Mosteshar, S. 29n
Mueller, P. 68n
multilateralism 83–4
Mutual Assured Destruction (MAD) doctrine 41–2

National Security Council, Action No 1553 (1956) 47n
NATO see North Atlantic Treaty Organisation
NATO CCD COE see NATO Cooperative Cyber Defence Centre of Excellence
NATO Cooperative Cyber Defence Centre of Excellence 53, 68n

NAVSTAR GPS satellites *see* Navigation Satellite Timing and Ranging GPS satellites
Navigation Satellite Timing and Ranging GPS satellites 44
Near Field Infrared Experiment (NFIRE) 43, 44
network centric warfare 33–4
New World Vistas: Air and Space Power for the 21st Century Report (USAF, 1995) 23–4, 44
NFIRE *see* Near Field Infrared Experiment
9/11 terrorist attacks 76
non-intervention principle 15, 83
non-kinetic force (electronic intrusions) 4, 6, 55, 83; and use of force 14, 16, 17; *see also* cyberwarfare; physical destruction (kinetic force)
non-nuclear weapons, offensive and defensive 38, 45
North Atlantic Treaty Organisation 20n; *NATO Strategic Concept* (2010) 16
North Korea 60
nuclear weapons 14, 36, 37; and *Anti-Ballistic Missile Treaty* 41–2; and *Limited Test Ban Treaty* 39–40; underground explosions 49n

Obama, Barack 15
O'Donnell, Brian T. 21n, 27, 30n
OODA (Observation, Orientation, Decision, Action) 91
Operations Other than War (OOTW) 27
outer space 6, 31–52; addressing a clear and present danger 72–82; *Anti-Ballistic Missile (ABM) Treaty* (1972) 41–3; assets *see* space assets; ban on military uses of 36; celestial bodies 32, 33, 36, 37; Committee on the Peaceful Uses of Outer Space (COPUOS) 73; conquering of (1950s) 1; damage caused by space objects on Earth's surface or to aircraft in flight 41; debris 80; direct military force in 33–4; *Draft Treaty on the Stationing of Weapons of any Kind in Outer Space* 74; Earth's orbit, ban on military uses 36; as fourth domain 4; indirect military force in 33, 34; intended use of technology 32; international law 32, 35, 37, 38, 46, 50n, 73; intersection on force and outer space law (*UN Charter*) 32–43; legal consequences of events/activities 3; *Liability Convention* (1972) 40–1; *Limited Test Ban Treaty* (1963) 38–40; meaning of 'peaceful' 31–2; militarisation and weaponisation of 4, 9, 33, 43–5, 47n, 74–5; military 'missiles' and civilian 'space launch vehicles' 38; moon 32, 37; network centric warfare 33–4; *Outer Space Treaty* (1967) 35–8; peaceful purposes *see* 'peaceful purposes' conundrum; race to space weaponisation 43; regime on Outer Space Law 9, 31, 34, 41, 75; space assets 4, 5, 6, 8n, 14, 34, 44, 80; space control 24; space force strength concept 15; space squadrons, US 24; space support 24; and Third States 40, 41, 42, 45, 62; as war theatre 25; *see also Outer Space Treaty* (1967)
Outer Space Conference (1960) 34
Outer Space Treaty (1967) 32, 35–8, 40, 47n, 48n, 72, 73, 75, 88n
Owens, W.A. 7n

Park, Andrew 73, 86n
peace: meaning of 'peaceful' 31–2; 'non-aggressive' versus 'non-military' 31, 32, 37, 72; 'peaceful purposes' conundrum 36–7, 39, 42, 45, 47, 72–6; re-orienting peace and security framework 76–8; Strategic Defense Initiative (SDI), 1983 36
'peaceful purposes' conundrum 36–7, 39, 42, 45, 47; resolving 72–6
Pentagon, US, Report (2007) 26
Perry, J.D. 48n
Petersen, J.H. 48n, 52n

physical destruction (kinetic force) 1, 4, 83; and cyberwarfare 59, 60–2; and use of force 9, 10, 13, 17
PLC *see* Programmable Logic Controllers 54
political independence 10
pre-emptive State actions, and self-defence 12, 14–15, 67
Primack, J.R. 87n, 88n
Programmable Logic Controllers (PLC) 54
proportionality, and self-defence 13
psychological warfare 56

Ramey, Robert 37, 41, 49n, 51n, 52n, 74–5, 86n
Ratner, M. 87n
Reagan, Ronald, 'Star Wars' program 36
Registration Convention see Convention on Registration of Objects Launched into Outer Space
Reijnen, G.C.M. 49n
restrictionist approach, self-defence rights 11, 12
Revolution in Military Affairs (RMA) 1, 23–30; cyber space (fifth domain) 25–7; grey areas between non-hostile and hostile operations 27; information RMA 2, 4, 6, 17, 71; outer space (fourth domain) 23–5
Rhinelander, J.B. 87n
Richards, P. 92n
Ricks, T. 29n
RMA *see* Revolution in Military Affairs
Romero, P.M. 7n
Rumsfeld, Donald/Rumsfeld Commission 25
Rusk, Dean 39
Russell, R. 19n
Russia 76, 84; suspected cyber assault on Estonia (2007) 2, 26, 53, 54, 63

San Francisco Conference (1945) 18n
satellites 1, 4, 8n, 62, 78; Anti-Satellite Weapons (ASATs) 14, 33, 34, 37, 42, 44; 'blinding' of sensors 34; NAVSTAR (Navigation Satellite Timing and Ranging) GPS satellites 44; Near Field Infrared Experiment (NFIRE) 43, 44; orbits as finite natural resource 79
SCADA *see* Supervisory Control and Data Acquisition
Schachter, O. 20n
Scheetz, Lori 81, 88n
Schiller, T. 7n
Schmitt, Michael 56, 69n, 92n
Schwelb, Egon 39, 50n
SDI *see* Strategic Defense Initiative, 1983
Second World War 10, 33, 77
Security Council, UN 59, 62, 78; *see also* United Nations
self-defence, right of States to respond in 9, 10–13, 35, 64, 85; anticipatory actions 12, 14, 67; 'inherent right' 11, 12; pre-emptive actions 12, 14–15, 67; restrictive versus counter-restrictive approach 11–13
Serabian, John 15, 16, 20n
service attacks, denial 62
Shaw, Malcolm 13, 20n, 67
Simpson, Gerry 10, 18n
Sklerov, Michael 57, 68n
'smart warfare' 1, 33
smokeless warfare 58–9
Soo Hoo, K.J. 92n
Sourbès, I. 49n
South Korea 60
Soviet Union (USSR) 32, 73–4, 79; *see also* Russia
space assets 1, 4, 5, 6, 8n, 14, 34, 44, 80; *see also* outer space
'Space Club' 76
space control 24
space force strength concept 15
space squadrons, US 24
space support 24
Spitzer, E. 86n
SSO *see* sun-synchronous orbit
'Star Wars' program (Reagan) 36
Stares, P.B. 48n
States: anticipatory or pre-emptive actions by 12, 14–15, 67; self-defence, right to respond in 9,

10–13, 35, 64, 85; space faring 76; territorial integrity 10, 18n, 59
statist defined military applications/processes 3
Stevens, Philip 92
stock market manipulation 62
Stone, J. 19n, 20n
Strategic Defense Initiative (SDI), 1983 36
strict liability approach, cyberwarfare 57
Stuxnet worm (2009–10) 53–4, 58
sun-synchronous orbit (SSO) 25, 79
Supervisory Control and Data Acquisition (SCADA) 53, 54, 60

Tallin Manual (*Tallin Manual on International Law Applicable to Cyber Warfare*) 58, 59, 62, 64–5, 66
TCA *see* Transformational Communication Architecture
telecommunications 3
territorial integrity 10, 18n, 59
territory, placing at another State's disposal 19n
terrorism, global 77
Third Department (China), Seventh Bureau 26
Third States 12, 26, 61, 76, 78; and outer space 40, 41, 42, 45, 62
Transformational Communication Architecture (TCA) 28
travaux preparatoires 10
Treaty Banning Nuclear Weapon Tests in the Atmosphere, in Outer Space and Under Water see Limited Test Ban Treaty (1963)
Treaty on Principles Governing the Activities of States in the Exploration and Use of Outer Space, including the Moon and Other Celestial Bodies see Outer Space Treaty (1967)
Tsagourias, Nicholas 58, 68n
twenty-first century warfare 1, 2, 4–5, 25

UN Charter see Charter of the United Nations (*UN Charter*)
United Nations: *Charter see Charter of the United Nations*; Committee on Disarmament 74, 75, 79; Conference on Disarmament (1986) 45, 52n, 75, 86n; Conference on Disarmament (2008) 79; First Committee 84; General Assembly *see* General Assembly, UN; re-orienting peace and security framework 77, 78; Security Council 59, 62, 78
United States: Air Force *see* USAF (United States Air Force); Cyber Command 16, 53, 68n; Cyber Consequences Unit *see* US-CCU (United States Cyber-Consequences Unit); Department of Defense (DoD) 2, 16, 24, 27, 57, 84; and international control of space activities 31–2; national security policy paper (2002) 24; *New World Vistas: Air and Space Power for the 21st Century Report* (1995) 23–4; 9/11 terrorist attacks 76; and *Outer Space Treaty* (1967) 34–5; Space Command *see* USSPACECOM (United States Space Command); Strategic Command 53; Strategic Defense Initiative (SDI), 1983 36; *US Quadrennial Defense Review* 27–8; West Point speech (2002) 76–7, 87n; withdrawal from *ABM Treaty* (2001) 43
uranium 53
USAF (United States Air Force): on counterspace operations 43; *New World Vistas: Air and Space Power for the 21st Century Report* (1995) 23–4, 44; space squadrons 24
US-CCU (United States Cyber-Consequences Unit) 54
USSPACECOM (United States Space Command), *Long Range Plan: Implementing USSPACECOM Vision for 2020* 24, 45, 52n
USSR (Union of Soviet Socialist Republics) 32; *see also* Russia

Vasiliev, Victor 79
Vienna Convention on the Law of Treaties (1969) 73, 86n
virus, computer 58
Vlasic, Ivan 32, 47n, 49n, 52n
vulnerability to attack 3

Wade, C. 50n
war theatre, outer space as 25
Watt, Arthur 83
Waxman, M.C. 10–11, 12, 18n, 19n, 20n
weaponisation of outer space 4, 9, 33, 43–5, 47n, 74–5; *see also* kinetic weapons

Weapons of Mass Destruction (WMD) 32, 36, 72
Weir, F. 87n
Weiss, E.B. 88n
West Point speech (2002) 76–7, 87n
Williams, C.D. 88n
Wilske, S. 7n
Wingfield, T. 7n
WMD *see* Weapons of Mass Destruction
Wong, N.C. 29n
worm, computer 26, 58; Stuxnet worm (2009–10) 53–4, 58

Zedalis, R. 50n